Praise For
The Gold Mailbox

"Schulman was only seven when she and her sister were all but abandoned by a mom whose priority was the new man in her life. When in time the man's true colors were revealed, abandonment might have seemed preferable. Recreated with astonishing detail and immediacy, this is a harrowing story of neglect and abuse, but ultimately an inspirational one. Schulman's insight into the power of family both for good and for ill is valuable and hard-earned."

—Martha Freeman, Author of 24 children's books including,
The Orphan and the Mouse; &The Secret Cookie Club

"*The Gold Mailbox* delivers a strong message — you can survive a painful childhood and go on to live a happy and healthy life. Schulman didn't win the parent lottery but her story affirms the power of love to help us overcome adversity. Highly recommend this deeply personal story."

—Deborah Drezon Carroll, Author of
Tales from the Family Crypt: When Aging Parents Die, Sibling Rivalry Lives; & Raising Amazing Children: While Having a Life of Your Own

The Gold Mailbox

A Memoir

Beth Schulman

OWL
PUBLISHING

Owl Publishing, LLC.
150 Parkview Heights Road
Ephrata, Pa 17522
717-925-7511

WWW.OWLPUBLISHINGHOUSE.COM

Cover Design by Zee Hayat
Edited by Justin Bog

PRINT ISBN978-0-9979-065-0-9
Library of Congress Control Number: 2016903529

Contents

To My Amazing Sister

Thank you for giving me the love, support and permission to write.

To My Dear Aunt and Uncle

Thank you for opening up your home and your hearts and showing me what it means to be loved unconditionally. I miss you every day.

To My Beloved Sons

Thank you for encouraging me to fulfill my dream of becoming a published author.
May you always work hard and have the courage to pursue your own dreams.

Prologue

MY MOTHER LURKED in every dark closet, under every bed, around every hidden corner. She was there, but not really there. I yearned for her love, her comfort, her protection. I was a young girl and I needed her. She'd show up, for brief periods, confusing me with her fleeting attention. She wore a mother mask, but I knew the monster that hid beneath it. After meeting the man she devoted her life to, she stopped wearing the mother mask. Her mask became one of silence and submission. The monster was still there, but now it had a partner. A bigger, stronger, more powerful monster had moved in. My mother became his minion.

Take my hand, dear reader and walk with me through the life-changing years of my childhood. Hold on tight as I share my moments of despair and hope, sister rivalry and sister love, abuse and care, death and emotional rebirth. Thank you for taking the journey.

Part One:
Queens

Chapter 1:
Home Is a Four-Letter Word

MOM WAS FULL of terrible surprises that year. First surprise came when she told Ellen and me she was divorcing Daddy. Then she surprised us by moving around all the furniture in our small garden apartment. Her big furniture move landed me and my single bed and plastic pink record player right in the middle of what used to be the eating part of the kitchen. When school let out she surprised us again by sending us to overnight camp for the whole summer. "There's a lake there and the counselors will teach you how to swim," she said, as if that was a good thing.

Swimming in a lake sounded awful. I imagined sharp rocks slicing my feet and slimy frogs hopping on my head. She told us the camp was in New Milford, Connecticut, which might as well have been on the moon, since I was only seven-and-a-half-years-old and didn't have a clue about life outside of Dale Gardens, the neighborhood in Kew Gardens, New York, where we lived.

* * *

Ellen and I sat next to each other on the camp bus heading back to New York. Camp had actually turned out to be a happy surprise. I felt homesick at first, but the counselors kept us so busy, going on nature walks, canoe rides, creating cool stuff in the Art Shack, there wasn't any time to think about the bad stuff. The best part about camp was no one knew about your life back home. They didn't know your parents were divorced or you lived in the kitchen. They didn't know your mom had gone a little crazy.

We sat right in the middle of the camp bus, underneath an emergency exit mounted on the ceiling. Our bus had high seats. They looked like they'd been fancy at some point, but were now worn and dirty. I rubbed my fingers on the armrest and it felt hard and spiky, like someone had spilled soda and never cleaned it up. My sneakers stuck to the sticky black floor speckled with flecks of gray. The bus smelled like burnt coffee and cigarettes. Ellen's hair, thick and soft like a bunny's fur, tickled my cheek when I leaned on her. Her dark brown hair fell well below her shoulders, just like mine. She spent a lot of time brushing her hair, every morning and every night. When I brushed my hair it hurt, so I didn't do it too often. It was really hot on the bus and we sat so close the side of her leg stuck to mine, like we were glued together. Ellen sat next to the window, one of the unspoken privileges of being the older sister. Her eyes were closed and she shifted in her seat and nudged me away. I felt the sweaty seal holding us together *pop* as she detached her leg from mine.

I looked around, trying to pass the time. I felt bored and itchy, having been in the same spot for over an hour. The tiny bathroom hidden in the back of the bus had a narrow door with an "occupied" sign on it. I recognized the two girls sitting across the aisle. They were from Bunk Three. That meant they were probably going into fourth grade. One year older than me. They had freckles sprinkled on their noses, rosy cheeks and knobby knees. They shared secrets and giggles, with heads bent and fingers busy braiding lanyard bracelets. I wanted to hear what they were saying, so I leaned forward a little. I couldn't hear a thing. Two boys sat in front of them. They were smaller than me, so they must've been from Bunk One. The boys were huddled together in a pile of sleep. One of them had a shiny bit of drool, hanging like an icicle from the corner of his mouth. I had an urge to get a tissue and wipe it away.

The brakes squeaked and the bus came to a halt in front of our YMCA. A wall of grown-ups lined the sidewalk where the bus parked. There were moms and dads, grandmas and grandpas, all waving and smiling. I stretched over Ellen, who was just waking up, and peered out the bus window. I didn't see Mom. She probably wasn't even there yet. She always ran late. I knew it really wasn't her fault since she didn't drive and had to rely on taxi cabs, buses and subways to get around. But, it didn't make it any easier. I hated waiting. I kept looking out the window and glanced over at the wide open parking lot. That's when I saw her leaning against an old white sedan, a lit cigarette hung from the side of her mouth, the one inch ash struggling to hang on. Her eyes were hidden behind big movie star sunglasses. Butterflies fluttered in my belly and my mind raced. We'd never owned a car and the thought of having one gave me goose bumps. Had Mom learned how to drive while we were at camp? I poked Ellen's shoulder and pointed out the window. She gave me a curious look and shrugged. We followed the other campers down the aisle and onto the street. The heat and humidity hit us hard. I wondered why it felt so much hotter in the city. I already missed camp with its cool breezes and refreshing dips in the lake. Ellen and I made our way over to the storage compartment under the bus. By the time we got there, most of the luggage had been cleared out by the camper's parents. The bus driver picked up our trunks and set them on the steamy sidewalk.

"Hey, girls, over here!" Mom waved, but made no movement toward us. Her body seemed to be attached to the old white car. Ellen and I grabbed the rope handles on the end of our trunks and dragged them across the parking lot. My trunk was so heavy, I could only move it a few steps before having to stop and rest.

By the time I made my way over to Mom, I was hot, tired and cranky. She spread her arms wide opened and gave us an "arms around the shoulders butt up in the air" hug. Not an arms wrapped tight, full frontal, "I really missed you and I'm so happy you're home" hug. If hugs could talk, hers would've said, "I'm not really a mother, I just play one on TV." It was a phony bologna hug. I peeked over her shoulder, half expecting to see Alan Funt and his crew from Candid Camera hiding behind a tree.

"I missed you girls' so much," she cooed, as if reading from a cue card.

Before I had a chance to ask about the car and where it came from, I noticed a little pug puppy with his long tongue hanging from the side of his mouth, his head peeking out the car window. When I got closer, the pug started barking like crazy and I jumped back.

"She likes you," I heard the voice coming from the driver's seat of the car.

A man, just a little taller than my five-foot mother, emerged from the old white sedan, holding the little dog under his arm like a football. His shirt stretched across his gigantic round belly, making him look like a pregnant lady ready to deliver. Bifocals perched on the end of his long, straight nose and three black wiry hairs stuck out of each nostril. His hair, what there was of it, was dark and swooped over from one side, attempting to conceal a large bald spot. I couldn't decide whether it was plastered with hair spray or just plain greasy.

"Girls, this is my new boyfriend, Saul."

I'd never heard Mom call someone her boyfriend. She and Daddy had been divorced for less than a year. After Daddy moved out, she'd go out a lot at night and sometimes wouldn't come home till early the next morning. But she never brought anyone home.

As I stood in the middle of the almost empty parking lot in the hot August sun, I couldn't help but think about Daddy. Did he know Mom had a boyfriend? Did he care? I wish he'd been the one to pick us up from camp. I wanted him to be the kind of dad who'd swoop in and save the day. But he wasn't that kind of dad.

Saul heaved our trunks into what should've been the back seat of his car. The back seat was actually missing, so the trunks sat right where the seats should have been.

"Hop in," Mom said in a sing song voice I didn't recognize.

Ellen and I awkwardly climbed into the back and sat on top of our trunks. Our backs were hunched and started to hurt right away.

"Where are we going?" Ellen finally asked.

"Saul wants to take us girls out to lunch. Isn't that so sweet of him?"

I was tired and mad and I wanted to be home taking a nap in my kitchen room. Saul pulled into the parking lot of a diner. Stiff and nauseous, I piled out of the car. Ellen took my hand and we followed Mom and Saul into the restaurant. I got hit with a blast of cool air and the temperature change made my head throb. We ended up in a booth, Mom and her new boyfriend on one side and Ellen and I on the other. I glanced around the half-filled restaurant thinking we probably looked like every other family, out for a nice lunch on a hot, August afternoon. Our waitress' frosty pink lipstick covered her front tooth and her bleached blonde hair pulled back in a tight pony tail revealed black roots.

"What can I get yous?" she asked clicking her gum.

"I'm not hungry."

Mom grabbed my knee under the table and gave me a "you better order something look," while still managing a fake smile.

"I'll have a grilled cheese," I muttered.

Mom started to talk in that high sing-song voice and didn't come up for air until our food was served. She babbled on and on about how she and Saul had dated all summer... the best summer of her life... Saul was a successful salesman... traveled to flea markets all over New York and New Jersey... very hard worker... very good money...

My head hurt. I imagined being at home in my kitchen room, listening to my only album, *Free to Be You and Me*.

I wish I felt free. Instead I felt trapped in a stupid restaurant with two strangers. Mom had changed into a different person while I was at camp. I whispered in Ellen's ear, "I want to leave," and she asked if we could wait for them in the parking lot. We walked in silence to the old white car with no back seat. I saw the little pug curled up on the front seat and wondered if she was dead. After all, she'd been stuck in the hot car for over an hour. I reached out tentatively to touch her. The tiny dog lifted her head and licked my hand and a wave of relief washed over me. She was still alive.

Mom and Saul walked out of the diner holding hands. Saul let go just long enough to smack Mom's butt. She turned red and started giggling. I looked away. It was all so gross.

Back in the old white car, sitting on top of our trunks, Mom started rambling on again... working with Saul at the Flea Markets... making great money... be gone from Thursdays to Mondays... since Ellen was so responsible she knew we'd be fine...

Saul pulled onto our street, carried our trunks up the stairs to our garden apartment and said goodbye.

We were finally home. But home, as we knew it, was gone forever.

Chapter 2: The Divorce

ELLEN AND I sat at the round table in the eating part of the kitchen. I'd just started 2nd grade at P.S. 99. It was a school day early in September and Ellen told me about the new gym teacher, Mrs. Miller, who made the bad kids stand in the corner. Mom poured milk over our Apple Jacks and said, "Daddy and I are getting a divorce." She said this in the most matter-of-fact way. She may as well have been telling us to wear a jacket or remember our lunch box for school. She poured herself another cup of coffee and just stood in the kitchen doorway, wrapped in her terrycloth robe with a strange far-away look in her eyes. I didn't cry right away. I was kind of in shock. I only started to cry when I saw Ellen blubbering next to me. I didn't ask any questions or ask her to reconsider. I knew my mother and when she made up her mind that was it. Period. End of story.

Mom had always been in charge in our family. She'd tell Daddy what to do and he would just do it. Every night he'd come home from work, kiss Ellen and me on the head and we'd all sit down for dinner. Mom would leave the table to put her feet up and smoke a cigarette and she'd tell Daddy to clean up the kitchen. He'd pile the dishes, carefully fold back the sleeves of his collared shirt and get to work. On the weekend, Mom gave him jobs to do around the apartment and he'd do them all without a peep. That's the way it'd always been in our family.

When Daddy came home that night, he followed Mom into their bedroom and closed the door. I couldn't hear what they were saying, but I figured Mom was telling Daddy about the divorce. After a while, I heard Daddy whimpering like a hurt little puppy. I ran into the bedroom I shared with Ellen. She lay on her bed staring up at the ceiling. I could tell she'd been crying from the look of her bright red nose and blotchy face. I climbed up next to her and when she wrapped her arms around me, my tears came, too. After awhile, Daddy came into our bedroom, holding a baby blue suitcase in one hand and his weathered briefcase in the other. He kissed us both and told us he was so sorry. He looked terrible. His eyes were puffy and his olive skin looked grey. He said he would be getting his own apartment, but he'd be by every week to see us. He blew his nose, wiped his watery eyes and just like that, he was gone.

Soon after Daddy left, Mom started acting weird. She hung signs in our apartment saying stuff like, "A woman needs a man like a fish needs a bicycle" and "You've come a long way baby." She changed all the living room furniture around every couple of days. When Ellen and I came home from school, we'd hear Helen Reddy's "I am woman, hear me roar" blaring on the record player and Mom would be stretched out on the couch, inhaling a Marlboro Light and panting heavily, her lip damp with perspiration, exhausted from her most recent furniture move. She'd beam, clearly pleased with her newest arrangement. "You like?" she'd ask. I'd try hard to curl my lips in a smile, but the truth was I hated all the changes. I wanted things to go back to the way they were. Then one Saturday morning, I woke to the loud banging of furniture moving. I got out of bed and found Mom pushing her full-sized mattress through her narrow bedroom door. She told me we all needed our own space so she decided to rearrange our bedrooms. I stood silently, wiping sleep from my eyes, while she dragged her mattress across the small foyer and into the bedroom I shared with Ellen. In the time it took me to pee and wash my hands and face, she'd pushed her dresser into our room. Ellen's bed went into my parent's old room and my single bed, small dresser and pink plastic record player got moved into the eating area of the kitchen.

Mom also started going out with friends late at night and sometimes wouldn't even come home until the next morning. She never talked about friends when she and Daddy were together. I had no idea where she was meeting these people and what she did with them. When I'd ask, she'd say she was finally living her life. She'd gotten married when she was 19-years-old and had Ellen when she was 20. Then I came along 3 and half years later. Now it was "her" time, she'd say. Sometimes it felt like we didn't even matter to Mom anymore. But then she'd surprise us with a treat from the grocery store or a new coloring book. I never knew what to expect from her.

Chapter 3:
The Dreaded Shopping Cart

AFTER SAUL DUMPED US alongside our trunks at the top of the steps of our garden apartment, he drove away in his old white sedan with no back seat. It wasn't long before Mom joined him on the road, working in Flea Markets all over New York and New Jersey. She and Saul would stop in once in awhile, but mostly we were on our own. I was 7-years-old, the youngest kid in my 3rd grade class at P.S. 99. I couldn't wait to turn 8 at the end of November. I started thinking about my life as pre-Saul and post-Saul. Pre-Saul, Mom did our laundry and made sure we had food in the fridge. But now we lived in the post-Saul era and we had to do everything.

Ellen and I took turns pulling the metal cart, stuffed with a black hefty bag filled with our dirty clothes. We walked up the steep hill to the Laundromat. A few leaves, oranges, reds and yellows, clung to the almost bare tree branches, but most were piled up on the ground, brown and crunchy. The dead leaves crackled under the wheels of the cart.

"My hands hurt."

"Well, it's your turn. I've been pulling the cart the whole way." Ellen snapped.

I dragged the cart slowly up the hill, trailing behind Ellen. I kept my eyes focused on the large roll of coins, bulging out of the back pocket of her Levis.

When we finally got to the Laundromat, next to the Corner Candy Store, my palms were on fire.

"Look at that." I put my hands in Ellen's face, showing her the hard, thick skin, on my palms.

"You're fine," she said.

Ellen got right to work, pulling the clothes out of the hefty bag and stuffing them into the washing machine. She sprinkled some Tide detergent on the top and slid two quarters from the roll in her pocket into the slot on the side of the machine. She stuffed the rest of the clothes into a second washer, sprinkled more Tide on top and slid two more quarters into that machine. A gigantic pair of men's white underwear slipped out of the hefty bag and fell to the floor. I bent down to pick them up and it wasn't until I had them in my hands that I noticed a long brown line on the back.

"EEEEEW, GROSS!"

I threw Saul's stained underwear toward Ellen. She ducked and they landed on top of the dust-covered plastic palm tree propped in the corner.

The sight of Saul's dirty underwear dangling from the plastic tree made Ellen and I crack up. We laughed so hard, our bellies started to hurt. It felt good to laugh. Ellen finally took a few steps toward the plastic tree, picked up the disgusting underwear between two fingers and used her other hand to hold her nose. She darted over to the washer and tossed them in.

"Nice work, Ellen," I said between giggles and gave her two thumbs up.

Still laughing, she grabbed my hand and pulled me out the door and into the Corner Candy Store. We each got an icy cold bottle of Yoo-Hoo. I picked out my favorite candy bar, the Charleston Chew and Ellen got her usual, a Snickers bar. Ellen opened the roll of coins from her back pocket and gave the cashier six quarters. We walked back to the Laundromat, sat on the hard plastic chairs and enjoyed our snack.

"Want to play hangman?" I asked after I finished my candy.

"Okay."

I ripped off the back of a magazine from the stack on the plastic table between our two chairs and picked up a tiny pencil with no eraser leaning against an ashtray overflowing with cigarette butts. I looked around the small, dingy room, searching for a word. We were the only people in the place which was a relief. I dreaded seeing anyone we knew. What if they asked where our mother was? Mom's life had become one big secret. My eyes found the word E-X-I-T above the door. I drew the hangman and put four lines for the four letters in the word.

Ellen guessed the vowels first.

"Is there an 'E'?" she asked.

How annoying. She already got the first letter. I made a clicking noise with my tongue, showing my frustration.

"How about an 'A'?" she asked.

I smiled smugly. "No 'A'," I added a head to the hangman.

"Is there an 'I'?"

I curled my lips and scrunched my eyebrows and wrote an "I"in the third spot.

Ellen examined the word carefully and then shouted, "It's EXIT!"

How did she get that so fast? I crumpled up the paper and tossed it in the trash can next to my chair.

"What are you doing? It's my turn to make up a word."

"Forget it. I don't want to play anymore."

"Don't be such a sore loser." Ellen got up and walked towards the row of washing machines.

I watched as she pulled the wet clothes out and tossed them in the giant dryer on the other side of the room. I got up slowly, knowing I should help. I hated the way Ellen always won every game we played. I pulled out a wet, heavy pair of jeans, shuffled over to the dryer and threw them in. I did this three more times while Ellen unloaded the rest. She put two more quarters in the machine which meant 40 more minutes to wait in this stupid place. I plopped down in the hard plastic chair, folded my arms over my chest and spread my legs out in front of me. Ellen, engrossed in a Cosmo magazine didn't even notice me pouting next to her.

When the dryer stopped, we stuffed the warm clothes back into the hefty bag and Ellen heaved the bag into the metal cart. She pulled the cart the whole way down the hill. She didn't even ask me to take a turn. Maybe she felt bad about being such a hangman show off. As soon as we got the cart up to our garden apartment, Ellen grabbed the book of food stamps Mom left on the kitchen counter and we were off to Key Foods. Doing the grocery shopping was even worse than doing the laundry. At least we used real money at the Laundromat. At Key Foods we had to pay with Food Stamps which looked like colorful paper money from a different planet. Everyone knew Food Stamps were for poor people. When Mom and Daddy were married they always had real money. But now we were poor.

Ellen and I pushed our metal shopping cart past the Corner Candy Store and the Laundromat, down two more blocks to the Key Food Market and I prayed we wouldn't see anyone we knew.

"Let's make this fast," Ellen whispered.

I followed her through the double doors into Key Food Market. Ellen folded up our metal cart and hung it on the back of the store's shopping cart. We headed straight toward the Cookie Aisle. I tossed in a package of Oreos and she grabbed a box of Graham Crackers. Ellen pushed the cart to Aisle 3 where we found the cans of Chef Boyardee ravioli, the long, skinny boxes of spaghetti and glass jars of tomato sauce. In the cereal aisle we added Apple Jacks and two boxes of strawberry Pop Tarts to our cart. On the way to the dairy section, we took a short cut down Aisle 9, Health and Beauty. The shiny boxes of hair color caught my eye and I stared up at the pretty blondes, brunettes, red heads, plastered on the front of each box.

Mom colored her hair once a month for as long as I could remember. Before I started school, I'd stay home during the day with her in our apartment. That's when we lived on the 13th floor of the high rise in Jamaica. Not the Jamaica surrounded by quiet sandy beaches and crystal blue waters, "the perfect getaway" advertised on TV. Jamaica, New York, surrounded by concrete, graffiti and strip malls. Mom colored her hair in the morning after Ellen left for school and Daddy went to work. She'd be wearing her silky peach nightgown, her bare feet planted firmly on our lime green bathmat, in front of the sink. I'd be in my pajamas, too, sitting on the toilet watching, as she opened the shiny box of Clairol Hair Color 7. The box had a lady on the front with beautiful long wavy hair. Mom's hair was short, cut around her ears and buzzed in the back. It came just to the middle of her wide neck. She'd take the stuff out of the box, two tubes, one white, one black, the plastic container with the squeeze top, a clear plastic bowl, a tiny brush with a red handle and one row of dark brown bristles, and the directions folded in a neat little square. She'd toss the unopened directions in the trash. I'd watch carefully as she squeezed the goopy white stuff from the white tube into the plastic container, followed by the goopy bright orange stuff from the black tube. She'd throw the tubes in the trash and they'd land right on top of the unread directions. Then she'd screw on the top of the container and shake. She'd shake and shake until the two liquids became one. She did this in silence, concentrating deeply, her tongue peeking out the side of her mouth, between clenched teeth. It was like watching a mad scientist conduct a cool experiment right there in the bathroom. She'd squeeze the concoction into the plastic bowl and hold the tiny brush between her pointer finger, the one she always bit down to the tip, and her thumb. Her other finger nails were thick, long and polished, but for some unknown reason Mom had a habit of biting one finger down till it bled. Dipping the bristles into the bowl of goop, she'd paint it with precise strokes on her hair, starting at the part and working her way down. The smell was something awful. It burned my nose and my eyes would tear. But, I'd stay on the toilet, hands tucked under my thighs, mesmerized by my mother's amazing skill. After she'd covered all her hair it looked like she had a pumpkin head. I'd follow her into the kitchen. She'd take the plastic white timer from on top of the stove and set it for 30 minutes. Then she'd pour me a glass of whole milk, add a nice long squeeze of Hershey's syrup and mix it all up with a long silver spoon, finishing it off with my plastic pink crazy straw.

"Let's go, Betty. I already got the milk. It's time to check out." Ellen's voice startled me.

I shook my head and rubbed my eyes, as if waking from a dream. I was back in Key Foods, Aisle 9 and Mom's bright orange hair was a million miles away.

While we unloaded our week's groceries onto the conveyor belt, I spotted Debbie Hanlon, the most popular girl in my class, standing beside a tall, thin pretty woman wearing pink lipstick and lots of mascara. Of course, her mom looked like a model. No surprise there. I turned my back, pretended to be studying the magazines in the rack, and prayed Debbie wouldn't notice me. It's not that Debbie and I were friends, with her being the most popular and me being the girl in the class who never spoke, but I still didn't want to be seen. I turned around slowly and let out a heavy sigh of relief when I saw Debbie and her beautiful mother leaving the store.

The cashier, a fat kid, with pimples covering his forehead, said, "That's $29.50."

Ellen pulled the book of Food Stamps out of her pocket, ripped out three paper bills and handed them over to Mr. Pimple Face. He rolled his eyes and scrunched his little pig nose. He took the Food Stamps tentatively, as if being poor was a disease he didn't want to catch. I felt my cheeks burn. I couldn't decide if I was embarrassed or just plain mad. Ellen remained completely calm. If she felt angry, she didn't show it. She opened our metal cart with one hand, placed the four brown bags filled with groceries inside it and walked out the door.

Chapter 4:
Consciousness Raising

AFTER UNLOADING the groceries, Ellen went into her bedroom and shut the door, her music cranked up loud enough for me to hear from my kitchen room. I lay down on my single bed and closed my eyes. The lyrics to *The Pretender* seeped through the crack in Ellen's door and filled my head. I began to think about the beginning of last year, when I was in 2nd grade and Mom and Daddy had just gotten divorced. That's when Mom started going to her weekly Consciousness Raising Meetings. I never knew what the meetings were for, but when she'd come home from one, she was always in a good mood. One time, she hosted a meeting at our apartment.

I held onto the shopping cart while she pushed it through Key Foods. Our cart was piled high with crackers, cheese, salami and lots of other treats for her friends. She let me get cans of potato sticks, boxes of Pop Tarts, bags of Cheez Doodles and packages of Malomars and Oreos. On the way home, she reviewed the rules for The Meeting.

"You can eat your snacks in my bedroom and watch as much TV as you want. But, the bedroom door needs to be kept shut and you must never, under any circumstances, interrupt The Meeting."

She sang, "Ain't No Way to Treat a Lady" and danced through the apartment as she set up folding chairs, TV trays and ashtrays. I chased after her like a hyper puppy.

"Betty, I'm tripping over you. Find somewhere else to be," she scolded.

But I begged to help and she sucked in a big gulp of air and let out a heavy sigh.

"Fine, go get me the salami from the fridge."

I smiled brightly and skipped over to the fridge, opened the door and grabbed the roll of Hebrew National Salami covered in red plastic wrap. It looked like a hot dog made for a giant. I was tempted to toss it to her like a football, but thought that might make her mad and I didn't want to ruin her good mood. Instead I placed it on the cutting board sitting on the counter. Mom took a sharp knife, peeled back the red plastic cover and began slicing the roll into thick circles. I counted the circles as she sliced. Ten slices by the time she was done. Then she cut each circle into 4 parts, making 40 triangle shapes. She told me to poke a fancy toothpick, the kind with curly colored cellophane on top, in the center of each salami triangle. I carefully placed each triangle on the shiny blue platter, until it looked like an ocean filled with a fleet of little salami sailboats. After she carried the salami tray out to the living room, setting it on one of the TV trays, she told me to get the box of Triscuits from the cabinet. I couldn't really read, but I knew the box was yellow and Triscuit started with a T, so it was easy to find them.

"Thanks, Betty Boop. You're a great little helper."

I smiled a big bright toothless smile. I'd just lost my third tooth, which left a big gap in my mouth and made me look like a funny looking Jack-o-lantern.

"Line the crackers up in nice rows, like this," she said, placing the first row of square crackers in a perfect line on the plastic rectangle-shaped platter painted with the yellow daisies. As she stood close to me, arranging the crackers, I breathed her delicious scent. She smelled like a combination of tobacco and raw crescent roll dough. When she finished, I counted 8 crackers on the platter. I reached into the box and counted 8 more crackers and lined them up, so they were right beside Mom's row. I fit in one more row of 8 and counted 24 altogether. Then Mom, like a professionally trained chef, shook the Cheez Whiz can and sprayed a dollop on each cracker. It looked like the crackers were covered in a field of bright orange flowers. She told me to open my mouth and surprised me with a long string of Cheez Whiz on my tongue. It tickled and tasted creamy, salty and delicious. Mom laughed then I laughed and pretty soon we were both out of breath from laughing so hard.

"We better get back to work, Betty. The women will be here soon," she said.

I helped her carry the remaining snacks, bowls of mixed nuts, Fritos and Ruffles Potato Chips into the living room. We spread the bowls out on the remaining TV trays and then placed two cans of French Onion Dip next to the Fritos and Chips.

The doorbell rang. She patted me on the bottom and sent me to her bedroom.

"But I want to meet your friends."

She gave me a familiar sharp look. I bowed my head and shuffled into her bedroom without argument.

For a while I sat by the door, eavesdropping. But the ladies talked in whispers making it impossible to hear anything, so I joined Ellen on the bed. She was already two episodes into a Happy Days marathon. At the commercial break Ellen got up to pee. She quietly opened the door and tiptoed out to use the bathroom. I stayed on Mom's big bed, flat on my belly, head resting on my folded arms at the end of the bed, legs methodically grabbing the pillow, picking it up and putting it down like some kind of crane. I would've stayed in that position, mesmerized by Fonzie straddling his motorcycle, sporting his cool leather jacket; black hair slicked back, thumbs up in the air, saying "Ayyy," if it hadn't been for the loud slamming of the door. I jumped, dropped the pillow between my feet to the floor and stared at the bedroom door. Ellen stood there, looking like she'd just seen a ghost.

"What's wrong with you?" I whispered, praying our mother wasn't on her way into the room to yell at us.

"Do you smell that?" she shouted.

I shook my head, "no" and told her to lower her voice. She continued pointing to the closed door.

"That smell is not from cigarette smoke, if you know what I mean!"

I had no idea what she meant, but I nodded and handed her a Malomar cookie, hoping it would calm her down.

"Does she think she's some kind of hippie teenager?" Ellen asked but I knew better than to give an answer.

Thinking back, it seemed like the Pre-Saul days were the good old days. I didn't care if Mom acted like a hippie teenager back then. At least she'd been home taking care of us.

Chapter 5:
Daddy

IT WAS WEDNESDAY night, Daddy's night. Every Wednesday Daddy picked us up for dinner and we'd spend every other Saturday with him, too. He arrived at our garden apartment, 5:00 p.m. sharp, rang the bell and we raced down the stairs to greet him. Daddy wasn't allowed to come into the apartment. That was Mom's stupid rule, and even when she wasn't home, Ellen and I didn't dare let Daddy in. It felt like she was always watching us, like at any moment, she could jump out from behind the bush in front of our garden apartment and catch us. Daddy waited in the small entry way of the apartment and gave us big hugs when we sailed down the stairs and through the door. Since he didn't have a car, we usually took the bus to Nathan's Hot Dog place where the thick cut French fries came in cups with a tiny, red three-pronged fork stuck in top. I liked to stab each fry with the fork and suck all the potato out of the center. If I did this in front of Mom she'd scold me for eating like a pig. Daddy never got mad about stuff like that. Sometimes on Saturdays we'd take the subway to Tad's, the cafeteria style steak place. They cooked the meat right in front of you and placed a big dollop of butter on top of each oversized baked potato. Daddy would cut my meat and pour A1 sauce on the side of my plate for dipping. I'd dig out the soft insides of the potato and Daddy would eat the skin.

At every meal we seemed to have the same conversation. It went like this:

Daddy: How's school?

Ellen and Me: Fine.

Daddy: Your education is the most important thing. You always need to work hard in school. Do your best.

Ellen and Me: We know.

The conversation always ended with Daddy blabbing on about how much he loved us, followed by a gigantic, earthquake of a sneeze. He'd grab his yellowed handkerchief from his back pocket, wipe his nose first, then his watery eyes. We never told Daddy about being left alone while Mom worked at the Flea Market, we didn't tell him about having to do the laundry and the grocery shopping all by ourselves. We didn't tell him about Saul. All that stuff would've made Daddy feel bad. We knew he couldn't do anything about it, so we just kept it to ourselves.

Daddy rarely took us to his apartment in Astoria, Queens. But tonight was special because it was the beginning of Spring Break and we were going to visit Auntie Esther and Uncle Benny in State College for Passover. We'd get to stay there until Sunday, four whole days away. Daddy picked us up at our Garden Apartment at the usual 5 o'clock time. He held his taxi and told us to hurry. We grabbed the little denim suitcases we'd packed for the trip and hopped in the cab. The cab pulled up to Daddy's apartment building 30 minutes later. It wasn't a tall high-rise like the ones in Kew Gardens. It looked more like a big brick house, but inside it was split into apartments. Daddy carried our little suitcases, one in each hand, through the heavy wooden doors leading to a wide open entryway. The hallway, shaped like a half circle, was lined with numbered doors. It reminded me of the game show, *Let's Make a Deal*. "Ok, Monty, what's behind door number two?"

Daddy walked so fast toward his door, the door with the number 6 on it, Ellen and I galloped just to keep up with him. He opened the door to apartment number 6 with only one key. Our garden apartment had two locks, a top and a bottom, but Daddy's only had one. His apartment was one big room, three large windows along one wall, a dresser against another and a single bed in the middle. There was a door leading to a tiny bathroom, but no separate kitchen or living room. Daddy's mini fridge sat next to his dresser and looked like it was made for a dollhouse. A hotplate sat on top of the dresser with a tea kettle on it. Our school pictures displayed in tarnished frames were the only other things on top of his dresser.

We sat on the edge of Daddy's perfectly made bed and watched as he carefully placed his folded clothes, one pair of ironed blue jeans, a collared long sleeve shirt and maroon sweater into the same blue Samsonite suitcase he'd carried out of our garden apartment the day Mom told him they were getting divorced. On top of that he put two pairs of white boxers, two pairs of socks, a hairbrush, a toothbrush held in a clear plastic tube and his short shaving brush, with a wooden handle and bristles that looked like they came from a horse's tail.

"Okeydokey Smokey," Daddy said as he zipped up his suitcase. "Time to hit the road."

Daddy called for a taxi and we found it waiting for us when we got outside. The driver, a small Indian man with a dark mustache took our denim suitcases and tossed them into the trunk. Daddy put his suitcase next to ours and the driver slammed the trunk closed. Daddy, Ellen and I piled in the back seat. The car smelled like smoke and I noticed the driver had a big fat cigar in his mouth. I watched the trail of smoke find its way through the tiny crack in the window. I squeezed Daddy's hand. My head felt dizzy from all that smoke. Just when I was about to throw up, we pulled into Penn Station. Even though it was 7 o'clock at night the sky remained bright. I loved that about the springtime. We waited half an hour for our Greyhound bus bound for State College, Pennsylvania, to arrive. It reminded me of our camp bus with the same tiny bathroom in the back, same sticky floor. The bus was only half filled, so Ellen took a whole seat to herself and Daddy and I sat across from her. Before the bus pulled out of the station, Ellen already had her head buried in her book, *The Secret Garden*. I wasn't much of a reader, so I hadn't packed any books for the trip. Luckily Daddy brought his special pen with the fancy lid tucked into his front pocket along with a tiny spiral notepad. We played tic tac toe, dots and hangman to pass the time. Daddy and I sang every word of "This Land is Your Land this Land is my Land" and then I fell asleep, leaning against Daddy's hairy arm. When I woke up we were in front of the Williamsport Bus Station. I rubbed my eyes and stretched my arms, surprised the five hour trip had gone so quick.

As soon as I got off the bus I saw Auntie Esther and Uncle Benny, their arms wrapped around each other's shoulders. The only light in the dark night came from the street lights lining the front of the bus station. The light shined down on their heads, giving them halos, like angels. We hadn't seen our aunt and uncle since last Passover, but they hadn't changed a bit. Auntie Esther's long dark hair still sat on the top of her head, twisted in a bun. Uncle Benny still only had a wisp of white hair bordering his mostly bald head. Auntie Esther wore a puffy black winter coat, hiding her wide hips and thick legs. I saw the outline of her fleshy upper arms through her big coat as she waved her arms and called "over here, over here!" The bus station was almost empty, but Auntie Esther continued to yell, clearly afraid we might not see them standing just a few feet away. I ran towards her, my cheeks rosy red from the cold night air and I wrapped my arms around her neck.

"Oh, Betty, look at you. You're all grown up," she said.

She wrapped me in her arms and my hair rubbed against her puffy coat. Her wool scarf scratched the top of my head. Auntie Esther's hug felt like home. Not like my Kew Gardens home, but the kind of home you see on TV shows like *The Waltons*. A nothing-can-ever-hurt-you kind of home.

We loaded into their little car and I pressed my face against the back window, marveling over the bright stars lighting up the night sky. We pulled into their driveway. Crystals of frost blanketed their front lawn. It seemed like it was still winter in State College. Like time moved slower there and spring hadn't yet shown up. We followed Uncle Benny onto the wide front porch and through the unlocked front door. The house was dark, except for one tiny light above the piano in the living room. Auntie Esther told us our cousins Ross and Brooke were already asleep so we needed to be quiet. Ross was sleeping on the futon in the basement, so we could have his room. Ellen and I climbed the stairs and headed into Ross' spacious bedroom. Three Penn State Football posters decorated the brown paneled walls and a big desk sat between the two single beds covered in blue and white bedspreads. I must've been real tired because I don't even remember getting into bed and falling asleep.

The next morning, I rubbed my eyes a few times before I remembered where we were. The round plastic clock with the letters PSU in the middle, read 11:00. I'd never slept so late. I looked over at the other bed and saw only ruffled covers. I tiptoed down the stairs and before I reached the bottom, I heard Uncle Benny's booming voice.

"Look who's finally awake!"

I peered into the kitchen and saw everyone crowded around the small kitchen table, cluttered with empty dishes covered in sticky syrup. Brooke got up and hugged me and Ross gave me a high five.

He said, "Yo, what's up little cuz?" Ross was so tall I had to stand on my tippy toes to see his big brown eyes and handsome smile. Brooke was 13-years-old, just like Ellen and Ross was 16.

"You must be starving, Betty," Auntie Esther said. "I'll make some more pancakes."

Uncle Benny opened the cabinet above the counter and started pulling things down. "Would you like some raisins, peanuts, cookies?" he asked.

Before I could say, "no thank you," Uncle Benny piled four oatmeal cookies on a plate in front of me and tossed a handful of raisins and peanuts on there, too. I picked up a cookie and started nibbling while Auntie Esther put water in the kettle and began to mix some more batter for pancakes.

Brooke, Ross and Ellen got up and bolted down the stairs to the basement leaving me alone with the grownups. Daddy sat next to me. He ruffled my hair and took a cookie from my plate. This kitchen was a happy place. Wallpaper with bright yellow and orange daisies covered the walls. The gold linoleum on the floor was worn in spots from so much traffic. A long bookshelf lined one wall, crowded with papers, cookbooks, a flower pot filled with pens, pencils, markers and hi-lighters. On the fridge there were loads of magnets from faraway places holding up school pictures of Ross and Brooke. The counter tops were overflowing with gadgets, a Kitchen Aide mixer, cans of tea and coffee, a few big ceramic containers stuffed with spatulas, big wooden spoons, metal whisks.

I finished my cookie and took a big gulp of apple cider Uncle Benny handed me. Auntie Esther put a mug of tea in front of Daddy and a plate of pancakes in front of me.

"Thanks," I said and poured a long stream of maple syrup on top.

"How are you, Issac?" Auntie Esther asked Daddy.

"Not great. It's been hard, really hard." Daddy took off his glasses and wiped them with one of the napkins from the table. "She's become impossible to talk to. She doesn't return my calls and won't even let me in the apartment anymore. What did I ever do to deserve this?" he said and pulled a handkerchief from his back pocket. He blew his nose and wiped his eyes.

I knew he was talking about Mom. My stomach churned, but I kept my head down and put another fork full of pancakes in my mouth. Auntie Esther reached across the table and squeezed Daddy's hand.

"Betty, go downstairs to the basement and play," Auntie Esther said.

"But, I want to stay here with you guys."

"Now, now, Betty Boop. Don't be a yenta," she said.

Daddy laughed, since he often called me his "little yenta." He said, "Come on now, little yenta, scoot."

Yenta means "busybody" in Yiddish. Daddy told me lots of stories about growing up with his older sister and brother, Auntie Esther and Uncle Murray. Their parents came from Russia and they grew up in New York on the Lower East side speaking mostly Yiddish.

"Oh, okay." I shrugged and headed towards the basement door.

Ellen and Brooke were talking and laughing when I came down the basement stairs. Ross was lying on the couch watching a Penn State basketball game.

Brooke said, "Hey, did you know your sister and I have magic powers? We can make ourselves disappear."

I knew she was trying to trick me, so I said, "Oh really? Prove it!"

They folded their arms and nodded just like the genie in *I Dream of Genie* and then the lights went out and before I knew it they were gone.

"Where'd they go?" I asked Ross whose eyes were glued to the black and white TV.

"I dunno," he said.

I raced upstairs and ran into the kitchen.

Daddy and Uncle Benny were gone and Auntie Esther stood at the sink, washing dishes. When she heard me stomp in, she turned around and asked what was wrong.

I told her about Brooke and Ellen tricking me and then I started to cry. She turned off the water, dried her hands on her apron and wrapped her arms around me tight.

"Oh, Bubbala!" she said, holding me close. My head rested on her chest and she felt warm and smelled like cinnamon. Her upper arms were soft as suede and they felt so good against my tear-stained face.

"Don't pay any attention to them. They think they're funny. Just be like a swan and let it roll off your back," Auntie Esther said.

Being in Auntie Esther's kitchen, bathing in her kindness made me feel like everything was going to be okay.

*   *   *

Two days later it was time to leave. Ellen and Brooke hatched a plan to hide our shoes so we could stay longer, but it didn't work and we piled back into Uncle Benny's little car and headed to the bus station. When I gave Auntie Esther one last hug, tears streamed down my face. As hard as I tried, I couldn't stop them.

"Oh, my sweet girl, you're so sensitive. Just like your Daddy," Auntie Esther said, removing her leather gloves so she could wipe away my tears.

I forced a smile and said, "Love you, guys," and followed Daddy and Ellen onto the big Greyhound bus.

Chapter 6:
A Tangled Mess

A FEW WEEKS after we returned home from State College, it was the end of the semester, which meant test time. I sat on the living room floor, my text books covered in brown paper bags, decorated with my penciled doodles of hearts and flowers, sprawled in front of me. I felt like I'd been sitting in that same spot for hours, just staring at the chapter on Rocks and Minerals in my 3rd grade science book. I couldn't tell the difference between a rock and a mineral and the big chapter test was tomorrow. I also had to memorize the eight times table for our weekly timed math quiz. Ugh.

School was never easy for me, like it was for Ellen. These days though, it seemed impossible. Mom used to help me with my homework, but those days were long gone. I got up, stretched my legs. My butt felt numb and my feet were all pins and needles from sitting so long. I took two giant steps toward the couch and plopped down. I shut my eyes and remembered the way it used to be.

Mom stood at the stove, frying up chicken cutlets in the heavy black pan, hot oil bubbled and popped like kernels of corn. I watched from my single bed in my kitchen room just three feet away.

"Mmmmm. That smells good," I said.

"Do your homework."

"I caaaaaan't. It's just too hard."

Mom narrowed her eyes, scrunching her thin, plucked eyebrows.

My belly tightened.

She turned off the gas burner, tossed the plastic spatula across the sink

and headed towards me at a quick pace.
"What seems to be the problem?" she said, obviously frustrated.
"I need to put these spelling words in sentences."
Mom grabbed the spelling list from my hand, tore out a piece of lined
paper from my spiral notebook and before I could utter another word, she
had scribbled down 10 sentences.
"Problem solved. Now copy these," she said flatly and handed me the paper.
"But that's cheating," I protested.

My stomach started to grumble. I missed Mom's fried chicken. I wish I'd just copied those stupid sentences. She'd only been trying to help. Maybe she felt like I didn't appreciate her enough. Maybe she got tired of being taken for granted. Maybe I was too busy thinking only about myself. Maybe that's why she followed Saul to the Flea Markets every week. Maybe she just wanted to get away from me. Maybe.

I got up and turned on the big TV that looked like a piece of furniture and sat on top of the sculpted olive green carpet. I adjusted the volume and started singing along with the Burger King commercial.

"Hold the pickles, hot the lettuce, special orders don't upset us, all we ask is that you let us have it your way."

The doorbell rang. I raced across the carpet and slid through the wooden hallway in my slipper socks. I headed down the stairs and opened the door.

Cheryl and Lori, Ellen's friends from across the street stood there. Cheryl chewed a wad of gum. She blew a big bubble and then sucked it back into her mouth with a pop.

"What's up, Betty Boop?" Cheryl asked, as she walked ahead of me, taking the stairs two at a time.

I hated when she called me Betty Boop. My real name is Beth. Ellen's been calling me Betty Boop ever since I was a baby. She named me after her favorite cartoon character. The name kind of stuck, but it was for family only. When Cheryl called me Betty Boop it felt like a big joke. I wanted to tell her to use my proper name, but instead I swallowed hard and followed her up the steps.

Cheryl's skin was a shade lighter than her dark brown hair. Her hair was parted in the middle and it hung like cooked spaghetti down past her shoulders. She sort of looked like an Indian. I tried to imagine her wearing a big colorful headdress and I started to giggle. "What's so funny, Betty Boop?" she asked clicking her gum. "Nothing."

"Where's Ellen?" Lori asked.

Lori was short for a 13-year-old. She and Ellen were just about the same height. Her red curls fell in front of her green eyes. Her eyes were the same color as mine. I pointed to Ellen's bedroom. The loud music from her clock radio made her door shake. Cheryl opened her bedroom door without even bothering to knock and told me to go out and play.

"We need our privacy," Cheryl said. I hated the way she put extra emphasis on the *pri-* in privacy.

I bet they were going to smoke cigarettes. Ellen started smoking about a year ago. I saw her smoking sometimes in front the Corner Candy Store with all her junior high friends. She'd usually put out her cigarette as soon as she'd see me. Did she think I was going to tell Mom? I wouldn't do that. Plus, Mom was barely around anymore, so how could I tell her anyway?

I slipped on my sneakers, didn't even bother to tie them, and left. I walked five doors down to see if Jenny was home. I saw her mom, Patti, sitting on the front steps of their apartment, smoking a cigarette.

"Hello, Beth. So nice to see you." Patti had a scratchy voice, the kind you get from smoking too many cigarettes, but to me, it sounded like beautiful music.

"Nice to see you, too."

Patti was the prettiest mom I knew and the nicest one, too. She had Farrah Fawcett hair and deep, dark suntanned skin. Her denim mini-skirt showed off her long muscular legs.

"Come, give me a hug," she said with an outstretched arm, her cigarette held firmly between her pointer and middle fingers. Her long nails were painted fiery red.

Patti wrapped her arms around me and my head got buried in her long thick hair. It smelled like sweet strawberries.

"Let me take a look at you," Patti said. "I think you've grown two inches since I saw you last."

I smiled shyly.

Just then, Jenny skipped out her front door.

"Hi, Beth."

"Hi." I tried to sound cheerful, but really I felt disappointed. I wanted Patti all to myself.

Jenny held a hairbrush, some hair bands and two ribbons.

"Hey there, sweets," Patti said lovingly.

"Come sit here," she pointed to the two concrete steps in front of her. Patti sat behind Jenny and started to brush her daughter's shiny black hair.

Mom used to brush my hair every night after my shower. I couldn't remember the last time she brushed my hair. That's probably why the back of my hair had become a tangled mess. I reached back self-consciously and felt the big knot. At camp, my counselor, Penny, had brushed the knot out of my hair, but now it was back and bigger than before. The day Penny brushed my hair and fixed it in a French braid was the best day of my whole summer.

It was Parent Visiting Day and since neither of my parents drove, they had no way to get to camp to visit. So, while the other kids showed their parents around camp and went out to lunch, Penny and I got to spend the whole day together. First we got into our bathing suits, lathered up with baby oil and took a canoe out on the lake. We paddled to the middle, put the paddles inside the boat, stretched out our legs and worked on our tans. After an hour or so, we paddled back and headed to the Art Shack.

"What color lanyard do you want?" Penny asked.

"How about purple and pink?"

"Nice choice," Penny answered as she cut two long strips of lanyard from the big spool hanging on a rusted nail stuck in the wall. She cut two more pieces for herself.

"Come on over here and I'll show you how to do the butterfly stitch." Penny patted the wooden bench sitting beside the big wooden table that had years of campers' initials carved into it.

I followed Penny's instructions and mastered the butterfly stitch. In just a few minutes, Penny and I were both wearing our new bracelets.

She took my hand and we skipped over to the canteen. Our bunk got to visit the canteen once a week. The canteen sold candy, chips and soda. Only the kids with money in their canteen account could buy something.

"What would you like?" Penny asked, hopping over the counter and

pulling out the boxes of candy bars.

"I don't have any money in my account."

"No biggie," she said. "On Visiting Day, everything here is free."

"Wow. That's awesome. I'll have some M&Ms, please."

Penny threw me a bag of M&Ms and she took a package of Twizzlers for herself. We walked around camp, eating our candy and talking.

"Are you looking forward to going into 3rd grade?" Penny asked.

"Sort of," I said. I didn't tell Penny how hard school was for me.

We stopped at the stone wall and sat on it. Penny kicked off her flip flops, pulled up her long gauzy skirt and sat crossed-legged. I followed her lead, untied my sneakers, and threw them down on the ground. Penny took off the small denim backpack she was wearing. She reached inside and took out a round brush and some colored hair bands. She put the bands on the same wrist as her butterfly lanyard bracelet.

"Can I do your hair?" she asked her voice as gentle as a breeze.

My heart began to flutter and my hands started to sweat. The Knot.

"It's okay," she whispered in my ear, so close I could feel her warm breath on my neck.

She started to brush my hair. Slowly. Carefully. When she got to the knot, my whole body tensed and I started to sweat again. We sat there in silence, Penny using little, gentle strokes to work out the whole twisted-up mess.

"There we go," she said, "feel that." She placed my hand on the back of my hair where the knot had been. My hair was soft and smooth.

"Thanks." I could feel a wet tear rolling down my cheek.

Penny divided my hair into three sections and started the braid at the top of my head and worked her way down to the middle of my back.

"Check it out," she said when she finished and handed me two pocket mirrors, so I could view both the front and back of my first French braid.

"Now you can really see those pretty green eyes of yours," she said. "You're a beautiful girl, Beth." Penny kissed my forehead and for the first time in my life I really did feel beautiful.

The brush sailed through Jenny's long, silky hair effortlessly. No knots. Patti made two high pigtails and finished them off with shiny pink ribbons, tied in bows.

"Jenny and I are meeting some friends for dinner," Patti said and gave me a hug goodbye.

"Yeah, I better get home for dinner, too."

I walked away knowing there was no one at home cooking my dinner. The sun was low in the sky and my stomach grumbled.

I opened the door and yelled up the stairs, "Hey, Ellen, what's for dinner?"

No answer.

I heard hushed voices coming from behind Mom's closed bedroom door. I tiptoed over and put my ear against it.

"I know, for a fact, it's a back massager," Ellen sounded annoyed. Then her voice got louder. "Stop it! Put that down! My mother has a bad back!"

Cheryl and Lori's laughter sounded like a pack of wild hyenas.

The door suddenly opened and I fell, head first, into the bedroom. The three of them didn't even seem to notice me.

"Chill out, Ellen. It's no biggie. It's actually kind of cool," Lori said as she and Cheryl headed down the stairs and out the door.

Ellen sat still on the edge of Mom's bed her pale face glistening with tears. I sat down next to her and put my arm around her shoulders. I saw her holding something that looked like a rocket ship.

"It's a vibrator!" Ellen blurted out and burst into tears. I rubbed her back and shoulders, trying to make her feel better, even though I had no clue what a vibrator was or why it was making her so upset. Ellen blew her nose and wiped her eyes. She got up slowly and put the vibrator in Mom's nightstand drawer.

"How about we open a can of ravioli for dinner?" Ellen said. Her voice sounded stronger. I wanted to ask her about the vibrator.

"Hey," I began, but then hesitated.

Ellen stopped and waited for me to finish.

I pushed away my curiosity, "I really love you."

Ellen put her arm around me and said, "I love you, too, Betty Boop."

Chapter 7:
Shower Scare

CHERYL AND LORI didn't come around for awhile after the vibrator incident. But after two weeks, they were back, hanging out in our garden apartment. It was Thursday night at 8pm and we were all in the living room watching *Chips*. Tony, the skinny black boy with the big afro, one of Ellen's other friends from junior high, came over with the girls. I wasn't a big fan of cop shows, but Ponch, the main guy on *Chips*, was really cute and watching TV with Ellen and her friends beat being alone in my kitchen room. I sat on the floor leaning against the couch, my legs straight out in front of me.

Ellen sat at my feet. She made a sourpuss face and said loud enough for everyone to hear, "Phew! Your feet stink, Betty! Go take a shower!"

"Shut up," I said, my cheeks burned with embarrassment.

I couldn't remember the last time I took a shower. I didn't care for showers because I always got water in my eyes. Plus, showers felt lonely. When I was little, Mom would fill the tub with bubbles and she'd sit on the toilet reading magazines. She'd let me play in the water until my hands and feet looked liked shriveled raisins. But, I knew baths were for babies, not for girls finishing up the 3rd grade.

I bent my head down to my toes, pretending to stretch my back, but really trying to get a whiff of my feet without anyone noticing. She was right. They really stunk. I got up and walked into my kitchen room. I wished I had a door, so I could have a little privacy. I sat on my single bed trying to figure out how to walk to the bathroom with just a towel wrapped around me and not be seen. I wouldn't care so much if it was just Cheryl and Lori, but Tony was in there and I didn't want HIM to see me. I decided to bring my pajamas with me and change in the bathroom after the shower. I quietly tiptoed past the living room and no one looked up. All eyes were glued to the car chase on TV.

I put my nightgown and towel on the toilet seat, turned on the water and stepped into the shower. Just before my foot hit the bottom of the tub, a gigantic black water bug ran across the bath mat, up the pink tiled wall and disappeared through a moldy crack.

I wanted to scream, but bit my lip instead. I hesitated before putting my foot on the worn out bath mat stuck to the bottom of the tub.

I picked up the Herbal Essence shampoo and noticed directions written on the bottle.

I read aloud, "Wash. Rinse. Repeat."

"Does that mean I'm supposed to shampoo twice?" I wondered.

"Hey Ellen," I called, "I have to ask you something. Come here for a sec."

A minute later the door opened.

"Is everything okay in there, Beth?" Tony asked in a high-pitched voice, pretending to sound like a girl. Before I could react, his big afro peered around the shower curtain.

"AHHHHHH!" I screamed, covering up as much as I could.

Tony ran out laughing hysterically.

I heard Ellen shout, "What the hell, Tony? Are you some kind of perv?"

Ellen came into the bathroom and handed me a towel.

"I'm so sorry, Betty. Tony is a dick."

She left and I stood there shivering. My heart raced. I felt mad and scared, but mostly, I felt like I couldn't move from that spot. I stood there, wrapped in a towel until I heard Ellen tell her friends to go home. She knocked lightly on the door.

"You okay?"

"I guess." I shrugged and tried to hold back my tears.

"I'm sick of Mom being away all the time," I said. "I miss her."

"I do, too. But, I'm really sorry about Tony. I won't let him come over here ever again," she promised.

Chapter 8:
Finding My Way Home

ELLEN KEPT HER PROMISE. Tony never came to our house again. Ellen's friend Kathy made a clubhouse in her apartment building's basement, which gave all of them a new spot to hang out. Every day after school, Ellen dragged me to the basement clubhouse.

"But, I don't want to go," I'd whine.

Ellen felt responsible for me. She didn't want to leave me home alone, but she didn't want to miss out on being with her friends, either. She'd always assure me we'd only stay for a little while. Unfortunately, that never ended up being true.

It was the beginning of June, but the heat made it feel like the middle of summer. The basement felt cool. The chill spooked me and gave me the shivers. The boilers hummed and cobwebs covered every corner. A few beanbag chairs were scattered about and a dirty, ripped up couch sat in the middle of the concrete floor.

I sat on the red beanbag chair and pulled a pencil and my long division math homework out of my backpack. I hated long division. I wrote my name and the date on top and then just stared at the 6 division problems. I started trying to solve the first one, but the loud hum of the boilers was too distracting.

"Can we pleeeeeeease go now?"

"We'll leave in five minutes," Ellen said, as she lit another cigarette and started making smoke rings.

Kathy, Cheryl and Lori lounged on the couch, puffing on their cigarettes, too. Tony sat, Indian style, right on the dirty concrete floor. I stuffed my math worksheet and pencil back in my book bag, put the straps around my arms and got up. I wandered around the basement, trying to pass the time. The only light came from a dim bulb hanging from the ceiling by a single wire.

I stumbled through a sticky spider web and stepped into some cold, muddy stuff. My foot sunk in the goop and I screamed, "Quicksand, I'm sinking in quicksand!"

Tony came running over and pulled my arm, hoisting me out of the yucky wet stuff.

"It's just some water," he said.

"Thanks," I said. I couldn't believe he was actually helping me.

Then just like that, Tony was back to being his mean old self.

"Hey Ellen, your bird-brain sister thought she was sinking in quicksand over there," Tony's voice bounced off the basement walls.

My heart sunk and I felt the heat rise up my neck, making my ears burn.

"Let's go, Ellen. Now!" I shouted.

Ellen barely looked up from the *Rolling Stone* in her hand.

"Why can't you just go by yourself, Beth? No one's stopping you?" Cheryl said.

I really hated her.

"I don't have the keys to our apartment," I stammered trying hard to come up with a reasonable excuse.

"I have a great idea," Kathy chimed in. "Ellen, give me your keys."

Ellen tossed our apartment keys to Kathy. She held up the keys and asked Ellen which was for the bottom lock. Ellen pointed to the one with the diamond-shaped top. Kathy took the frosted peach nail polish she was using to paint her toenails and put a little peach dot on the diamond-shaped key.

"The one with the dot is for the bottom lock." Kathy handed me the keys and smiled smugly.

I glared over at Ellen, who said she'd be home in 5 minutes. I stormed out, swinging my backpack behind me. The sun had set and Austin Street was all dark.

"Fuck you, Ellen," I shouted into the black sky. Then louder, "I hate you!"

Then on the top of my lungs I shouted all the curse words I knew, "FUCKSHITDAMNIT!"

I was all alone on Austin Street and I liked the way my voice sounded, shouting curse words into the night. I started to skip. I suddenly felt light and airy. When I reached our garden apartment I saw the reflection of the gold mailbox shining against the entrance door.

I could picture Mom standing there, proudly holding a paintbrush dripping in gold. It was shortly after she'd moved my single bed into my kitchen room. I'd just walked home from school when I saw her.

"Hey there, Betty Boop, come look at our beautiful new mailbox!" she shouted and I was sure the entire neighborhood was staring at us through their sealed windows. Her short orange hair looked freshly dyed and her bangs were held back by several silver bobby pins, exposing her large sweaty forehead.

I peeked into our entryway. Our mailbox, which had been black like all the others on our street when I left for school, had been transformed into a sloppy gold mess.

"What were you thinking? It's absolutely awful!" I yelled and ran upstairs to my kitchen room. I sobbed into my pillow. Why did she have to ruin everything? Daddy was gone and everything was different. Our mailbox was the only thing that remained unchanged. And now that was gone, too.

I felt Mom's warm body lean up against mine.

"I'm sorry," she said. "I wanted to make it pretty."

She rubbed my back with her strong hands and then lifted my shirt up. She started to scratch from the tippy top to the way down bottom. It felt so good, like all the angry parts of me were melting away and only the good stuff was left.

"It's not that bad," I muttered and drifted off to sleep.

The same gold mailbox I'd once detested welcomed me home, like a beacon of light. I approached the front door and turned the knob. It opened without the key. We must've forgotten to lock it. I started laughing, finding the whole mess totally hilarious.

When I got up the stairs, I walked straight ahead to my kitchen room and over to my record player. My "Free to Be You and Me" record was already on the turn table, so I put the needle on the first song and turned up the volume. I plopped down on my single bed and listened to "Mommies are People." I imagined Mom scratching my back from the tippy top all the way down to the very bottom. I fell asleep before the song ended.

Chapter 9:
Puberty Unleashed

I DON'T REMEMBER the actual day Saul moved in. Like a sneaky cat, he crept up from behind and pounced, landing right in the middle of our garden apartment. First his electric razor showed up on the sink in our tiny bathroom. Then his newspapers covered the living room floor. Before I knew it he was sitting at our round kitchen table, in nothing but boxers and a wife beater t-shirt slurping down a cup of black coffee. Ellen had been complaining to mom about all the time she was spending away from home. So, mom's solution was to move Saul in. Ellen told me if she knew Mom and Saul were a package deal, she never would've complained in the first place.

On a Tuesday night, I found myself alone with Saul in our garden apartment. Ellen was at Cheryl's house working on some school project, Mom was taking a nap (she seemed to be napping a lot, ever since Saul moved in) and I was sitting at the kitchen table, trying to get my homework done. From my spot at the table, I could see Saul sitting on the toilet like a king on his throne. His legs were spread, dingy underwear around his ankles, glasses on the tip of his nose. He held a folded newspaper in his right hand and a pen in his left. Why he insisted on doing the crossword puzzle while sitting on the toilet, I'd never know. I couldn't stop myself from staring at his gigantic stomach which sat on his lap like an oversized baby.

Saul had a bunch of ridiculous rules. Like, "the open door" rule. We were no longer allowed to shut our bedroom door or the bathroom door. Of course, I didn't have to worry about my bedroom door, since my room was part of the kitchen and it had no door. But, keeping the bathroom door open was totally weird. Saul said we were a family now and families didn't hide anything from each other. Families had no secrets. I couldn't understand how taking a pee in private counted as a secret, but I knew better than to challenge Saul. I'd seen him get pissed off and it wasn't pretty. He could be real nasty.

One time when Mom was carrying some shopping bags up the stairs, she just kind of collapsed. Ellen and I were watching TV and by the time we got there, Saul had hoisted her over his shoulder and carried her into their bedroom, like a sack of potatoes.

When he came out of the room, I asked, "Is she okay?"

Saul freaked out and screamed, "If you girls weren't so goddamn lazy, maybe your mother wouldn't have fallen. Next time, get off your goddamn asses and help her with the bags!"

Just remembering how he screamed at us, how his face turned bright red and how the vein on the side of his head pulsed gave me the chills. My stomach hurt deep down inside and I felt beads of sweat gathering under my hair at the base of my neck. I got up and walked into my kitchen room. I put my pillow in the middle of my bed and laid face down on top of it. I stretched my arms out and closed my eyes. I felt weak and tired, but I couldn't fall asleep. My belly hurt more than it'd ever hurt before. I got on my knees and bent my head all the way to my blanket. The pain got worse. It felt like someone was stabbing me from the inside. Like a sharp knife was slicing through my belly, all the way to my back. I felt something warm and wet between my legs. I stood and sat right back down. I was so dizzy I thought I might pass out. I sat on the edge of my bed, spread my legs wide apart and looked down. A red spot, the size of a quarter, stained my white sweatpants.

I ran to the bathroom, praying Saul was finished in there. *Screw you Saul*, I thought as I slammed the door shut. I pulled down my white sweatpants and pink panties. My heart raced when I saw all the blood.

"Oh my God! I'm bleeding!" I yelled out loud.

The wooden floor squeaked as Saul's heavy footsteps approached the bathroom door. I heard his fists banging hard against the hollow door.

"Why is this door closed?"

Before I could muster a response, the door swung open and Saul's body filled the doorway. He stood with his hands on his hips and his big stomach grazed my face.

"Well, well, well. Look at that. Little Betty has become a woman." Hot tears stained my cheeks. "It hurts!"

"It's just your period, not a goddamn terminal illness."

Saul's words cut right through me.

I pressed my legs together and bent over, trying hard to ease the pain and hide the patch of curly black hair that had started to grow down there. I heard the front door open and prayed Ellen would come and save me.

"Give your little sis a hand in here," Saul called to Ellen. "And keep your voices down, your mother's sleeping." With that, he sauntered back into the bedroom.

Ellen came into the bathroom and looked down at my blood-stained underwear on the tiled floor.

"Holy shit. You got your period."

"It hurts."

"I'm like practically the only girl in 7th grade who hasn't gotten her period and now my 9-year-old sister has gotten it before me. I can't believe this!"

I sat there on the cold toilet seat, stomach cramping and started to cry. Ellen reached over and rubbed my back.

"I'm so sorry, Betty. This isn't your fault. Here take one of these."

She handed me one of Mom's Kotex Maxi Pads. I pulled the adhesive strip off, as I'd seen Mom do before and stuck it to my blood-stained underwear. I pulled my underwear on and it felt like a gigantic diaper. I hobbled into my kitchen room, eased myself into my bed and wept into my pillow. I thought about walking over to Jenny's house and telling her I just got my period. *I'm probably the only girl in the whole 4th grade who has her period. What if Jenny tells someone? Could I tell Patti? Would she tell Jenny?* I got that all-alone feeling. I curled on my side and fell asleep.

The next day, I got up early and checked my pad. It was covered in a brown stain. I tiptoed into the bathroom. The apartment was quiet. I rolled the pad up in some toilet paper and buried it, along with my stained underwear, at the bottom of the trashcan under the sink. I took two pads from the package, stuck them under my pajama shirt and crept back to my kitchen room. I put on a fresh pair of panties attaching one of the pads to the inside, before pulling them up all the way. I hid the other pad in my book bag underneath my binder and finished getting dressed. Ellen and I sat at the round kitchen table, eating our bowls of cereal in silence.

"How do you feel?" Ellen finally asked.

"I'm fine," I lied.

When I got to my 4th grade classroom at P.S. 99, I saw Ms. Moyer, the haggard-looking speech therapist standing by the door.

"Good Morning," she said flatly.

"Morning," I mumbled, looking down at the floor.

I'd forgotten it was Wednesday, dreaded speech therapy day. I put my coat and book bag in my cubby and followed Ms. Moyer down the hall. Her pudgy feet stuffed into high heels made a *clip clop* on the worn out wooden floor and her pony tail flipped back and forth like a horse's tail. I had to gallop just to keep up with her. The big pad rubbed between my legs. I wondered if it made me walk funny. *Will Ms. Moyer notice? Will she ask what's wrong with me?* My palms started to sweat.

We arrived at Ms. Moyer's little room, a converted closet, and she told me to sit down. Her face was expressionless, as usual. I assumed she hadn't noticed the big old bloody pad stuck between my legs. I sat down at the little table and watched as she pulled her suit jacket over her large stomach.

"Have you been practicing your *j* sounds?" she asked.

I nodded yes, even though I hadn't practiced at all.

"Okay, then, let's hear you say 'juice.'"

"Goose." I tried hard to make the *j* sound.

"Ju, Ju, Ju," she chanted.

"Gu, Gu, Gu," I repeated.

After several minutes of this, I could tell Ms. Moyer was getting frustrated. She peeled off her suit jacket, revealing a rose-colored, silky blouse with big sweat stains under the arms. The blouse had short sleeves and Ms. Moyer's big, thick arms looked like they belonged to a football player.

"Let's try working on the diagraphs," she said. "Ch, Ch, Ch."
I couldn't get my lips and tongue to cooperate and my *chs*
sounded nothing like Ms. Moyer's. And I couldn't stop thinking
about the blood between my legs. If Ms. Moyer knew what I was
going through, she'd probably take pity on me and just send me to
the nurse so I could lie down.

As if she read my mind, Ms. Moyer told me I'd worked hard
enough for one day and gave me some scrap paper and an old coffee
can filled with markers.

"Here, you can draw."

Even though half the markers were missing lids and all dried
out, I felt relieved. I could stop making those ridiculous sounds and
just sit quietly. I made swirly marks and smiley faces all over the
paper while Ms. Moyer sipped her can of Tab. She flipped through
the pages of a Sears catalogue, where the models wore matching
panties and bras. I looked down self-consciously at my t-shirt, pulled
tight across my chest. I had an undershirt on under it, which did
absolutely nothing to conceal my round breasts. Even though I'd cut
the arm holes in all my undershirts so they'd fit, I knew I should be
wearing a bra. No one in my 4th grade class had started developing
yet, and I hated how my body was changing at warp speed. The hair
on my legs had gone from peach fuzz to thick dark fur. It matched
the dark hair covering my arms. I just wanted all of it gone. Why
couldn't I be like everyone else?

On the walk home from school I made the decision. I'd ask Mom
to show me how to shave my legs. I charged up the stairs, right into
her bedroom, before I could lose my nerve. Mom and Saul were in
her bed, under the covers. Saul's chest hair peeked over the top of
the blanket and Mom's shoulders were bare. I wanted to run out of
there, but I took a deep breath and stated my case.

"My legs are really hairy and I need to shave. I'm sick of wearing
knee socks all the time to cover up the hair. And..."

Saul cut me off. "Oh, here we go again with the hysterics. We
will not allow you to shave your legs. End of discussion."

I wanted to scream, "What do you mean, *we*? Why should you
have any say at all?" I wanted to shake my mother by her bare shoulders
and say, "Speak up! You shave your legs why can't I shave mine?"

I wanted to, but I didn't. Instead, I just stood there glaring at Saul. I tried to make eye contact with Mom but she seemed to be hiding behind Saul's big stomach. Saul broke the silence. "If you start shaving, the hair will come back thicker and darker and you'll have to do it every day. Go get the tweezers. I'll show you how to pluck the hairs out so they won't grow back."

"You have got to be kidding."

Mom popped her head up and finally spoke. "It's true, Betty. Once you start shaving the hair just grows back thicker than before."

I stormed out of the bedroom and went right towards the bathroom, slamming the door when I got there. Screw Saul and his stupid rule. I picked up Mom's pink daisy razor sitting on the side of the tub. My hand shook. I stared at the blade. It looked really sharp. I decided to do a trial run on a patch of arm hair. The razor scratched against my dry skin. Seeing the bald spot on the front of my arm, right above my wrist, made me panic. I set the razor down on the side of the tub exactly where I found it. I ran to my kitchen room and cried into my pillow. Defeated again.

Chapter 10:
Creasies

JENNY AND I were walking home from school when she asked if I wanted to sleep over her house, and of course, I said yes. It was a Friday afternoon and Mom and Saul were spending the weekend in New Jersey to work at a big flea market there. Ellen had gone over to the clubhouse with her friends. She rarely dragged me over there anymore which was fine by me. I was a 5th grader now and didn't need a babysitter anymore.

I followed Jenny into her apartment and saw a set of keys attached to a Lucite rectangle with the letters P-A-T-T-I engraved in it, sitting on the kitchen counter. My heart raced.

"Hi there, girls. How was school?" Patti asked when she rounded the corner with a basket of laundry leaning on one hip.

She looked beautiful, as always. Her blue eye shadow, thick dark mascara and shiny red lipstick made her look like a model. She worked as a secretary in a doctor's office a few mornings a week and I bet all the guys who came into the office fell in love with her. Patti put the basket down and gave Jenny a big kiss, leaving a perfect imprint of her red lips on Jenny cheek. Jenny wiped it off immediately with the back of her hand and said, "Come on, Beth. Let's play in my room."

Jenny was in 4th grade, one year younger than me, but she bossed me around like she was the bigger kid. I didn't mind. It beat sitting around the musty basement clubhouse or worse, sitting alone in my kitchen room.

"Let's play house," Jenny said. "I'll be the mom and you can be the big sister."

"Okay." I knew most 5th grade girls had stopped playing with dolls, but I still loved dressing up all of Jenny's babies. She had over a dozen dolls, in various sizes. I had one doll I got when I was like 5-years-old. I lost the outfit it came with a long time ago, so the doll lived under my bed, naked and untouched.

"You need to dress and feed your baby sister, while I get ready for the party," Jenny said handing me one of the bigger baby dolls. She pulled out the large container of baby clothes from under her bed and sat in front of the full length mirror hanging from the back of her door. Jenny riffled through Patti's makeup bag and started applying eye shadow and glossy lipstick.

I opened the container and sorted through all the cute little outfits folded and stacked neatly in piles. Patti saved every outfit Jenny wore when she was a baby. I recognized an outfit from one of the many pictures of baby Jenny hanging all over their apartment. There wasn't a single baby picture of me hanging in our apartment. Sometimes I wondered if I ever was a baby.

I chose a flannel pink onesie covered with yellow ducks and dressed the baby. Then I pulled out a tiny jar of baby food from a smaller container stored under Jenny's bed. Patti was such a cool mom. She bought real baby food for Jenny's dolls. I opened the jar of apple sauce, pretended to feed my baby sister, while stealing little samples for myself. It was smooth and didn't have much taste, but it felt good sliding down my tongue. Patti came into Jenny's bedroom and I quickly pulled the little spoon out of my mouth, praying she hadn't seen me.

"Dinner is served," she said with a giggle.

Patti let us make ice cream sundaes for dinner and she pulled out the sofa in the living room that converted to a bed. Since their apartment had only one bedroom, Patti slept on the pull-out couch. Jenny and I shared the pull-out bed and Patti slept in Jenny's room. Sometimes when I couldn't fall asleep in my kitchen room, I'd think of Patti sleeping in her sofa bed. Neither of us had a proper bedroom. The thought of having something in common with sweet, beautiful Patti made me happy.

Jenny and I cuddled under her favorite quilt while we watched the movie, *The Bad News Bears*, on TV. Jenny's quilt was another thing she'd since she was a baby. I rubbed the worn out faded material between my fingers and got goose bumps. The quilt was covered in creasies. A *creasie* is the soft, creased spots on my pillow. I rubbed my lips against the creasies every night to help me fall asleep. I was tempted to rub my lips on Jenny's creasies, but didn't want her to think I was drooling on her special quilt.

The phone rang. Patti got up from the rocker in the corner where she'd been filing her nails.

"Hello? Yes, Gaye, she's right here, watching a movie with us."

Long pause.

"I'm very sorry. I didn't realize you were home tonight. I'll send her right away."

Click.

Hearing my mother's name spoken aloud sent my heart racing. I climbed out of the sofa bed and met Patti in the kitchen. I started to cry. Big, hard, body-shaking sobs. I just couldn't stop myself. Patti wrapped her tanned arms around me and held me tight. She stroked my tangled hair. I tried to speak, but my words got stuck in my throat.

"The movie isn't over...Jenny's quilt is so soft...don't want to go..."

Patti told me to get my shoes on and she disappeared. By the time my sneakers were tied, Patti came back, holding something in her fist. She stuffed it in my coat pocket and told me to run home. The brisk air made my breath float through the night like a smokestack. I ran home, peeking back only once and saw Patti wrapped in an oversized terrycloth robe, watching me from her front door.

I opened the door to my apartment, tiptoed up the stairs hoping to slip right into my kitchen room without being noticed. No such luck. Mom stood at the top of the stairs, like a watch dog, wearing a sleeveless nylon nightgown. The fabric of her nightgown was so sheer, it as if she were standing there naked. I looked down to avoid staring.

"Look at me!" she bellowed, "and tell me who the fuck you think you are? I am your mother, not Patti. Are you listening? What did you tell her? Why does she think I wasn't home...?"

She continued her rant, but I stopped listening. I stared down at the spaces between the hardwood planks on the floor, wishing I could just melt right through those cracks.

"Are you listening? I said you owe me an apology!"

I managed a meek, "I'm sorry" and shuffled past her toward my kitchen room. When I heard her bedroom door slam, I threw my coat on the floor, got into my flannel Scooby Doo nightgown and crawled into bed. My head hurt and my heart pounded. I laid there for several minutes, my head, so full of questions, it hurt. Why was Mom home anyway? Was Saul home? Where was Ellen?

Then, I remembered. I jumped out of bed, grabbed my coat from the floor and reached into the pocket. I held Patti's gift tightly in my hand, but wouldn't allow myself to take a peek until I got back under the covers. I opened my fingers slowly, one by one, and found a piece of square fabric attached to a diaper pin, an oversized safety pin with a plastic top. The fabric came from Jenny's quilt. I rubbed it between my fingers for a long time. Finally, I curled my legs close to my chest, slid my left arm under the pillow and brought the fabric to my lips.

Chapter 11:
M.S.

I WOKE in the middle of the night to the sound of something scratching in the kitchen cabinets. I held on tight to the piece of blanket attached to the diaper pin. I rubbed it against my lips, hoping it would get me back to sleep.

Scritch, scratch, scritch, scratch.

The noise got louder.

I threw my covers to the floor, stomped out of bed and turned on the light. With the fluorescent kitchen light shining down on them, three gigantic rats, beady eyes and long thin tails, scurried for cover.

"AAAAAAHHHHHHHHHHHHH," I screamed and jumped up on my bed. "HEEEEEEEEEEELP!"

Saul appeared in the kitchen door wearing yellowed briefs, a tight white t-shirt stretched across his big belly, black dress socks barely covering his thin pasty calves. The patch of hair, usually brushed over and sprayed in place on top of his head was standing straight up. He looked ridiculous and I had to bite my lip to keep from laughing out loud.

"What's going on in here?"

I found it hard to respond, still shocked to see Saul standing there in his underwear.

"Umm, we've got rats! I saw three big ones running across the floor!"

"You're such an idiot! They're just field mice. Now stop making such a racket. You've upset your mother enough for one night. She needs her sleep."

Saul turned off the kitchen light and left. I slowly got back under the covers and laid there wide awake, feeling certain the rats were going to climb up on my bed if I closed my eyes.

The next morning, I woke to the smell of fried salami and eggs. Mom stood just four giant steps away from my bed, still wearing the flimsy nightgown from the night before, holding a cigarette in one hand, spatula in the other.

"Good morning, Betty. Glad you finally decided to wake up." Mom's voice sounded cheerful and not at all like the witch who'd greeted me the night before.

"I'm really sorry about last night," I began but before I could finish, she fell and hit the floor, with a great big *thud*. The spatula flew through the air and the burning cigarette landed on the linoleum floor. I jumped out of bed and ran over. I carefully picked up the cigarette and put it in the olive ashtray on the counter next to the stove. Then I turned off the burner and knelt down next to her. I shook her arm. "Mom, you okay?"

A tiny stream of blood oozed from a cut on her forehead. She must've hit it on the corner of the counter.

"Mom," I yelled louder, "Wake up!" I felt dizzy and nauseous.

Saul came rushing in and screamed, "What the fuck is going on?"

His booming voice seemed to wake her. He put his hand out; Mom reached for it and he pulled her up.

"Don't just stand there, get some ice!" Saul's voice startled me.

I jumped and hurried over to the freezer and put some cubes in a paper towel. Mom reached up to the cut on her head and I dabbed it with the ice. The bleeding had stopped. Saul grabbed the ice from me and put it up against my mother's head.

"Stop fussing," she said. "I'm fine."

She finished making breakfast and we all ate at the round table in the foyer and it was like it never happened. Saul got up first.

"Hurry up, Gaye. We're already late," he said, grabbing the newspaper and heading to the bathroom.

Mom told Ellen and me to get the dishes cleaned up and she disappeared into her room. After they left, Ellen told me the reason they'd come home early from the Flea Market.

"Mom had a bad episode at the Flea Market," she said.

"Episode? What does that mean?"

"You know, from her Multiple Sclerosis."

"What's that?"

"I can't believe she's never told you. She's had it since you were born. It's like a disease that makes her dizzy and shaky sometimes. Haven't you ever noticed?" Ellen asked.

I hadn't noticed. I was totally clueless. How could my mother have had this crazy disease for all these years and never bothered to tell me? How come Ellen knew? Why was I always the last to know everything?

Shortly after finding out about Mom's M.S. (that's what she started to call it) her episodes became more frequent. Maybe she'd been having the episodes for a long time, but I just hadn't been paying attention. I began to watch Mom more carefully and started to learn the signs of an upcoming "M.S. episode." She'd stop whatever she was doing, grab onto something stable- like a wall or a counter. Her face would get all pale and she'd start sweating like crazy. Then she'd take some pills, lay down for a few hours and when she got up, it was business as usual.

Chapter 12:
The Flea Market

SAUL HAD BEEN living with us for over two years, but it seemed like forever. It was hard to remember a time he hadn't been there. I was in the final weeks of 6th grade at P.S. 99 and had already started counting the days until I'd be off to YMCA camp for my 5th summer away. Saul insisted we start to help at the Flea Market since Mom's M.S. had gotten worse. He acted like her M.S. was our fault. When Mom held her arm and leaned against the wall, Saul would scream, "Look at how you are making your mother suffer!" It seemed like every time Saul opened his mouth, he was blaming us for something. I really hated him.

Mom woke me at 4:45am.

"Come on, Betty, rise and shine."

I rubbed my eyes and peeked out the window. The dark sky made it look like the middle of the night. I'd never been up so early. Mom got busy making sandwiches in the kitchen while I got dressed. I watched her peel the hard boiled eggs, place them in the bowl and mash, mash, mash. Then she spooned globs and globs of Hellmann's Mayonnaise into the bowl. With a fork, she whisked it altogether until it became bright yellow and extra creamy. She placed eight slices of Wonder white bread on the counter and piled mounds of egg salad on each piece. Then she covered the egg salad up with another piece of white bread, cut each one diagonally and stacked them all in a brown paper bag.

"Wear a sweatshirt," she said, "it's cold this early in the morning."

We crowded into the cab of Saul's big white work truck.

My mother was in one of her "everything is great" moods.

"You girls are going to love working at the Flea Market," she said, handing Ellen and me an egg salad sandwich. "Now eat up. You'll need lots of energy today."

"It's too early to eat," Ellen whined.

It was hard for me to resist Mom's enthusiasm. It'd been a long time since I got to eat one of her yummy egg salad sandwiches. I thanked her for making it and gobbled it up in just a few bites. Then she started singing. Her voice was high and squeaky, like some jolly cartoon character.

"When the red, red, robin goes bob, bob bobbin along...," she sang, clapping her hands and moving her head from side to side.

Ellen looked at me and rolled her eyes.

Saul pulled the big white truck into a wide open lot. There were lots of other trucks around, with people pulling out tables and boxes. Mom asked Saul if she could show us around. He gave a grunt that she must've taken as a "yes." She grabbed our hands and started swinging our arms like we were little kids off to our first day of preschool. She brought us to a stand a few feet away, where half a dozen guys, wearing cut-off shirts threw out crates of fruit from a truck that looked a lot like Saul's.

"Hey guys," Mom batted her eyelashes and waved. "Come meet my girls. This is Ellen and this is Beth."

A guy with big muscles and a red bandana wrapped around his head walked toward us. He reached out and shook our hands.

"Yo, nice to meet you."

The other guys just waved as they continued to unload the wooden boxes filled with peaches, apples and melons from their truck.

"Now let's go see Molly and Abe at their cheese table," Mom said, acting like Julie McCoy, cruise director of *The Love Boat*.

Molly and Abe looked like someone's grandparents. They both had white hair, wrinkled faces and big, toothy smiles. They sat next to each other on canvas director chairs, behind a long counter covered in cheese.

"Great to finally meet you girls," Molly said. "Are you hungry?"

Before we could answer, Molly told Abe to give us a sample of the smoked Gouda.

Abe sliced a piece of the cheese for me and Ellen. I popped the whole piece in my mouth. It tasted awful, nothing like the thin orange squares wrapped in cellophane we had at home. I swallowed and forced a smile, trying to make a good impression.

The last person we met was The Pickle Lady. That's how Mom introduced her.

"Girls, this is the Pickle Lady."

The Pickle Lady sat on a tiny stool and because she was really fat she looked like a gigantic mushroom. The stool was her stem. A big wooden barrel filled with pickles sat beside her. The strip of dark hair on her upper lip looked like a fuzzy caterpillar and I wondered if she used to work in the circus. She put on plastic gloves and reached into the big barrel, pulling out two pickles. They looked small in her thick hands, but when she handed them to us they were huge.

"Enjoy," she said in a deep voice.

I noticed her left eye twitching and I felt sorry for her.

"Thank you," Ellen said and nudged me with her elbow.

"Yeah. Thanks a lot," I said.

It felt so weird to be standing in a big open lot eating an oversized pickle at 6 o'clock in the morning.

"Ok, girls, time for us to get to work," Mom said and we followed her back to our stand.

Saul had already set up the tables and unloaded the bakery goods they sold. She told us to line up the black and white cookies, linzar tarts and elephant ears on big metal trays. Being around all the sweet stuff made me feel light-headed and hungry.

"What the fuck is this?" Saul's angry voice rang in my ears.

He pointed to a broken black and white cookie sitting on the tray in front of me.

"We can't sell that shit if it's broken!"

After Saul walked away, Mom whispered in my ear, "Put the cookie under the table and you can eat it later."

Her voice was unfamiliar, kind and gentle. I snuck the cookie over to where Ellen stood and gave her a piece. It tasted more like cake than a cookie. I wanted to savor it, but instead gobbled it down quickly before Saul could catch me.

Mom walked over to me and Ellen and I was afraid she saw me eat the cookie. Even though she said it was okay, you never knew with Mom. One minute she'd be all loving and nice and the next minute she'd be yelling like a crazy person. I wiped my mouth with the back of my sweatshirt sleeve. She handed each of us a green apron. She tied it around my waist and told me to keep the money in the front pocket. She handed me and Ellen a roll of coins and a wad of $1 bills. Then she pointed to each cookie and pastry and rattled off prices. It wasn't until that moment that I realized I was going to have to wait on customers. Math was my worst subject. I couldn't even add and subtract in my head, how was I going to figure out how to make change? What if I made a mistake?

The customers began lining up at our table at 7:30. I hid behind Ellen for most of the morning. I got bags from under the table and handed out napkins, but luckily Ellen took care of the money. I watched my sister wait on customers with confidence and ease. She was a natural. She always remembered to say *thank you* and *have a nice day*. The steady stream of customers tapered off around 10:30.

Mom told us the morning crowd was gone and it would get busy again after lunch.

"Get yourselves something to eat and come right back," she said handing Ellen a $5 bill.

Ellen and I walked up and down the endless rows of tables covered in t-shirts, towels, sunglasses, shoes, socks, night gowns, mood rings, key chains, dog leashes, cat toys, baby blankets. I grabbed the hood of Ellen's sweatshirt so I wouldn't get lost. We stopped to get a hot dog with sauerkraut. Pickles at 6 and hotdogs at 10:30. The Flea Market felt like a separate world with its very own time zone. After we ate, we walked over to the produce stand. Bruce Springsteen blared from the boom box on top of the produce guy's truck. Ellen started singing along. She knew the words to every Bruce Springsteen song. The guy with the red bandana and the big muscles came towards us.

"How's everything going?" he asked winking.

"It's okay," Ellen said. "I can't believe how many people are here."

"Yeah, this is the time of year everyone comes out. Been shut in all winter and they're just dying to spend some money."

I stared at the big, colorful cross painted on his bulging right bicep. Ellen asked for two peaches and handed him a dollar bill.

"No need. It's on me, girls."

"Well, thanks. Umm….have a good day," Ellen said.

"Will do, little lady."

As we walked away, Ellen gave me a peach and whispered, "Oh, my God, he is so cute. Did you see his tattoo?"

Saul popped out of nowhere and said, "You think the tattoo on his arm is impressive, you'd really love the one on his dick. It says 'fuck me' and you can only read it when his cock is big and hard."

How long had he been standing there watching us?

We acted like we didn't hear him and walked toward our cookie table. For the rest of the day, I couldn't stop staring at the produce guy with the cross tattoo, wondering if what Saul had said was true. Saul was such a jerk. He put that dirty picture in my head and now that it was there I couldn't erase it.

Part Two:
Brooklyn

Chapter 13:
Bye-Bye Kitchen Room

THE BUS pulled out of the camp parking lot, marking our 5th summer away at the YMCA camp in New Milford, Connecticut. We were headed back to reality. I couldn't muster any excitement about returning home. Home had become a dreaded place where I spent all my energy trying to avoid Saul and his temper. Ellen sat with her friends from the Senior Division in the back row and Jodi and I sat closer to the front. Jodi, my best friend from camp, had long legs, long arms and perfect caramel-colored skin. I loved her wild chocolate-brown hair best of all. Not in a million years would I ever be that beautiful. It grew out, not down and puffed out like cotton balls.

"Do you think you and Eric will see each other during the school year?" Jodi asked.

"Probably not," I shrugged.

"I mean, after all, I live in Queens and he lives all the way in the Bronx."

Thinking about Eric gave me goose bumps. He was my first official boyfriend. He was going into 6th grade and I was going into 7th but since I was young for my grade and he was old for his, it felt like no big deal. His shoulder-length hair, feathered back just right, reminded me of Scott Baio. I had a picture of Scott Baio hanging on the wall above my bed in my kitchen room. I cut it out of Jenny's *Teen Beat* magazine. I could get lost in Eric's big dark brown eyes. My palms started to sweat just thinking about him. When Eric asked me to try out for the camp's production of *The Wizard of Oz* I said sure, even though the thought of being on stage in front of the entire camp made me want to wet my pants. Eric got the part of the cowardly lion and I earned the role of one of the mean monkeys who hid in the forest, waiting to scare Dorothy and her friends. After the play ended, Eric and I spent all our free time together at camp.

I looked over at Jodi. "And anyway, I don't think Eric wants anything to do with me now that he's met my father." It happened right after breakfast on Visiting Day.

Eric and I sat on the boat dock our bare feet dangling in the lake. We were waiting for his parents to arrive, when he asked, "Who's that?" He pointed to a man walking up the steep hill from the camp's parking lot. I put my hand above my eyes, shielding the sun. I squinted, trying to make out the faraway figure.

"What a freak! He's wearing a long-sleeve shirt and corduroys. Does he not realize it's 90 degrees out? Gross, I can see his armpit sweat stains from here," Eric mocked.

I couldn't think of anything cool to say, so I shrugged and watched the sweaty guy in the corduroys huff and puff up the hill. As he got closer, I realized the freaky dufus with the sweat-stained pits was my father.

"That's my dad," I mumbled in disbelief.

"Are you serious?" he sounded shocked and disgusted.

I hopped off the boat dock and ran toward my father.

"Surprise, Betty Boop!" his voice was way too loud. I looked back to see if Eric was watching, but he was already gone.

"What are you doing here?" I snapped as my dad tried to hug me.

"I thought you'd be happy to see me," he said, taking off his glasses and wiping his eyes and sweat-stained forehead with his handkerchief.

I spent the entire day moping. While Ellen showed my dad around camp-the bunks, the lake, the pool, the Art Shack and the Nature Center, I trailed behind kicking rocks. While all the other campers were out eating McDonald's with their parents, I was stuck eating tuna casserole with Dad and Ellen in the camp's dining hall. We were the only people in the whole place.

As I sat on the bus, recalling that awful day, I started to feel guilty. Dad had taken a train, a bus and a taxi just to get to camp to see me and I'd been a total brat. I decided as soon as I got home, I'd call him and apologize for the way I'd acted.

"I can't wait to start Junior High School this fall. It'll be totally cool to have a locker and switch classes." Jodi's voice brought me back.

"Yeah, I think Junior High will be a blast," I lied.

"My mom promised me when I started 7th grade I could get a puppy," she said. "I hope she takes me to the pet store to pick one as soon as I get home. Do you have a dog?"

I said, "I actually have two. One is a Great Dane. Her name is Samantha and the other is a bulldog named Governor. We call her Govey for short."

"Wow, you're so totally lucky," Jodi squealed.

I remember feeling lucky when Saul first brought Govey to our garden apartment last year. She had a smooched face and a stubby tail and she made lots of grunting noises. I thought she was adorable. Saul told us she'd be a good watch dog and she'd keep us company when he and my mom went to work at the Flea Markets. He'd been right. She barked every time someone came to the door or even when she heard kids playing outside. At night, when the mice would start their scampering in the cupboards of the darkened kitchen, I'd heave Govey up on my bed, which was no easy feat. She was small, but bulky, like a butterball turkey. She had a little indent between her eyes, right above her flattened snout. My finger fit in there perfectly. I'd rub that spot right between her eyes and Govey would snort, showing her pleasure. I felt safe and protected from the scary mice that lived in the kitchen cupboards.

As much as I loved Govey, taking care of her was a pain. We had to remember to feed her twice a day and walk her, too. Ellen and I would usually go together. We'd walk her across the street to the railroad track. When Ellen was off with her friends, it was up to me to take Govey out all by myself. I hated walking her at night. I'd hear noises in the darkness and get totally spooked. When Govey would start to whine, wanting to go out after dark, I'd tell her to just poop in the house. She'd whine a while longer, but with my encouragement, she'd eventually squat in the corner of the living room and do her business right there on the sculpted olive green carpet. I'd get a paper towel and pick up Govey's poop in one hand, while squeezing my nose between two fingers with my other hand. Then I'd run to the kitchen and bury the poop deep down under all the trash in the garbage can. It was pretty disgusting, but it was better than going outside in the dark by myself.

Then one day a few months after we got Govey, Samantha arrived. Samantha was Saul's dog. I'm not sure who'd been taking care of her while he was living in our house, but out of the blue, Saul dumped her on us. "Now Govey will have company," Saul had said.

But, like all the things Saul brought into our garden apartment, the dogs were a big mistake. Taking care of Samantha was 10 times harder than caring for Govey. She'd jump up and nearly knock you over on account of her size. Her long tail wagged so hard the end of it split open and splattered blood all over the walls of our garden apartment. The walls stayed like that, stained with Samantha's blood. I actually felt sorry for Samantha and her bloody tail, but at the same time I hated her. She was Saul's dog and it wasn't fair we were stuck taking care of her. I often wondered whatever happened to the little pug Saul had when we first met him. Knowing Saul and his terrible temper he probably got annoyed with her one day and threw her in some dumpster on the side of the road.

"Oh, my God, we're back already." Jodi's voice startled me.

I looked out the window and saw our YMCA right past the next traffic light. When the bus pulled into the parking lot, I saw Saul's big white truck double-parked in the bus lane. It stood out amongst all the cars and station wagons. Just like our gold mailbox, it was a scream amongst whispers. I longed for the days when it was just Mom picking us up from camp an hour late in a taxi. I hated Saul's big white truck. I felt embarrassed to be seen in it. The back of the truck was always filled with loads of crap. Sometimes there were trays of cookies, sometimes it had racks of used jeans, other times it was piled high with day old donuts and loaves of bread.

I gave Jodi a big hug when we got out on the pavement.

"See you next year," Jodi waved as she made her way over to her mother.

I waited for Ellen to get off the bus. We found our trunks and dragged them over to Saul's truck.

"Hey girls," Mom said hopping out and giving us each a quick hug. Saul stood right beside her. He hugged us too, but his hug lingered and it felt strange. We all squeezed into the front seat of the truck.

"Where are we going?" Ellen asked. "This isn't the way back to Kew Gardens."

Mom stumbled over her words. "Oh, um…there was a flood in our apartment so we…um…won't be going back there."

"What do you mean?" Ellen shouted.

"Luckily Saul kept his house in Brooklyn, so we're all going to move in there." My mother announced this horrifying news in the same excited tone you'd use tell someone you'd just won the lottery. My stomach felt like it'd just been punched.

"Our whole lives are in Kew Gardens-our friends, our school, everything," Ellen's voice trembled.

"You'll make new friends. It's a good time for a move. You'll be starting High School and Betty will be starting Junior High. It'll be a fresh start. We'll be a real family in Brooklyn."

"What about Dad?" I asked feeling tears well up in my eyes.

"Your father will just have to come visit you at our new home in Brooklyn," Mom's voice shifted, now sounding terse and annoyed.

Ellen and I both started to cry. Saul told us to stop acting like babies. He said it was time for us to grow up. I held onto Ellen's hand the whole way to Saul's house in Brooklyn. We'd never been there before. We got out and stared at the twin brick house on Hendrickson Street. A full flight of concrete steps lead up to a porch. It didn't look too awful from the outside, but as soon as we walked in, a foul musty smell hit us like a ton of bricks. To the left was a kitchen and what appeared to be a living room sat to the right. The entire place had no electricity, so it was dark. All the blinds and windows were closed.

The living room was long and narrow. A large desk, overflowing with papers, took up the whole corner near the window. A big black vinyl chair, the kind with wheels on the legs, sat behind the desk. In the other corner, there was a double bed and a metal TV stand holding a small television. A wooden chair sat beside the TV. No couch. No coffee table. Not even a single TV tray.

Saul led us through the strange living room toward the two bedrooms. The two rooms were filled with racks and racks of clothes, like jeans, coats, blouses and dresses. Saul told us he'd been using this place as a warehouse. One of the rooms was so crowded with boxes and old clothes, the door wouldn't even open the whole way. Part of the ceiling sagged and had a big water stain on it. In the other bedroom a single bed was set up right in the middle, surrounded by more racks of hanging clothes.

"This is your room, girls," Saul pointed to the overcrowded room with the single bed.

Ellen squeezed my hand hard. We hadn't let go of each other since getting out of the truck. Saul dumped our trunks into our new bedroom and told us to unpack. He disappeared out the bedroom door. I suddenly realized I hadn't seen the dogs anywhere in the house.

"Where do you think Govey and Samantha are?" I asked Ellen.

She shook her head and said, "I don't have a clue. But I know one thing for sure-wherever they are, has to be better than this."

We went to bed early because we didn't know what else to do with ourselves. The sun hadn't even set when Ellen and I climbed into the single bed. Ellen put a sheet between us and told me to stay on my side. Mom didn't come in to say goodnight. We lay flat on our backs, wide awake, staring up at the ceiling. The ceiling had huge spots where the paint curled at the edges and looked like it might fall right off. I forced my brain to see a picture in the peeling paint, like when you look up at the sky and see cool shapes in the clouds. But I saw nothing. Just a dingy ceiling covered in peeling paint in a place I already hated.

Chapter 14:
The Thompson Family

THE NEXT MORNING we piled into the white truck and drove to a nearby YMCA. Saul said we'd be using the YMCA showers, since the water hadn't been turned on in his house yet. I felt trapped in a nightmare. Ellen whispered, "This sucks," and reached for my hand.

We sat close, squeezing our hands together, until Saul pulled the truck into the parking lot of the YMCA. This YMCA was nothing like the one in Queens. The brick building, covered in graffiti, had empty bottles and discarded bags from McDonald's lining the entrance. An old guy wearing a wool hat, even though it was the end of August, leaned against the building sipping from a bottle wrapped in a brown bag. I tried to avoid staring as we entered through the big double doors. Saul strutted up to the front desk and Mom, Ellen and I followed behind.

"Hi, there," he said to the old lady sitting behind the desk. She had short white hair and glasses hung from a chain around her neck.

"My name is Saul Thompson and I need to add my wife and kids to my membership."

I wanted to shout, "We do not belong to him! He isn't even married to our mother!" But, instead, I stood there, quietly outraged.

"No problem, Mr. Thompson."

The lady with the white hair and glasses around her neck took our pictures with a Polaroid camera for our membership cards. For a split second I thought I should ask for a hairbrush, so I could look presentable for the picture. Then I thought it didn't really matter. Nothing mattered anymore. It all seemed absolutely hopeless.

"Sign here," she said handing me a pen and pointing to a line on the bottom of the card.

Underneath the line I read, Beth Thompson, typed in small black letters. My hands started to sweat. As I signed Beth Thompson in my neatest cursive, I felt like I might throw up. My whole life was one big lie. The old lady handed me a map of the facility. Little did she know we were only there to use the shower.

Chapter 15:
Junior High

MOM SHOWED ME where I'd meet my bus, on the corner of Hendrickson and Avenue U the night before school started. I felt completely lost, standing at the bus stop, amongst all the grownups on their way to work. In Brooklyn, there were no school buses for Junior High and High School kids. All the students took public transportation. I'd never taken a public bus by myself and I felt beyond nervous. I wasn't the only kid waiting at the bus stop. There was a small pack of girls, dressed in blue and green plaid skirts, crisp white button-up shirts, knee socks and shiny black Mary Janes. I'd later learn they were Catholic School girls, going to Saint Mary's High School. I'd also learn that Catholic school girls didn't associate with the public school kids. They stood in a huddle and acted like I didn't even exist.

The bus pulled up and I followed the uniformed girls up the stairs. I watched them flash their school badges at the driver, and I did the same. If you had a school badge you didn't have to pay. The crowded bus, filled with men smoking cigarettes, old ladies gripping canes and young mothers holding drooling babies, smelled like a sweaty locker room. The Catholic school girls made their way to the back of the bus, but I stayed close to the front. Since there were no empty seats, I positioned myself behind the driver and held tight to the silver pole behind his seat. Every time the bus stopped my body swayed forward and I'd hear "Weebles wobble but they don't fall down," play in my head.

The Catholic School girls got off and I started to panic. Had I missed my stop? I leaned over to the driver and asked how much further to Madison Junior High.

"Next stop," he said.

I saw the sign for the school and my heart beat so loud I thought everyone on the bus heard it. I walked off and started towards the building. There were tons of kids hanging out in front of Madison Junior High. The school was three times the size of P.S. 99 and all the kids looked like they were way older than me. Most of them wore sneakers, jeans and t-shirts with decals saying stuff like "Mellow Out" and "Keep on Truckin'." I wore chinos and a maroon and beige-striped sweater I'd found in one of Saul's used clothing boxes. The sweater had a little hole under the right armpit, so I concentrated on keeping my right arm plastered down by my side. I felt totally overdressed and made a mental note to wear jeans from then on. After I pushed my way through the crowd, I wandered around the halls for a while until I found the school office. When I walked in there were two kids lined up at the big counter. I stood behind them.

The secretary greeted the first boy with a smile and a "what can I do for you?" The boy handed her a note. "So, you need to leave at 2:30 for a dentist appointment, huh?"

"Yup."

"Good luck. Hope you don't have any cavities," the secretary said with a smile.

The next in line was a tall girl with long arms and a face filled with pimples. She spoke in a whisper. The secretary bent over the desk to hear what she was trying to say.

Then it was my turn.

"Hello, there. What can I do for you?"

"I'm new."

"Welcome. Did your family just move here?"

"Yes. From Queens. Well, Kew Gardens, actually. It's a little neighborhood in Queens."

"Oh, yes, I know Kew Gardens well. I have some cousins over there. Nice area."

I attempted to say, "Yes it is," but the words got stuck in my throat.

"Did your dad get a new job here in Brooklyn?"

I didn't dare tell her my dad lived in an efficiency apartment in Astoria and I'd been taken to Brooklyn by my mother and her nasty boyfriend against my will.

I nodded and mumbled, "uh huh."

She asked me my name and when I started to say Beth Schulman. I stopped. What if Mom had registered me as Beth Thompson? My heart raced.

"Excuse me?" she said.

I cleared my throat and said, "My name is Beth Schulman."

"Give me one minute," she walked away from the desk.

I watched her go through a doorway leading to a smaller office. I paced the length of the counter trying to think of what I could say if she didn't have a Beth Schulman registered. Beads of sweat dripped from my temples and my stomach started to ache.

"Here we go, Beth," she said, handing me a piece of paper when she returned. A wave of relief washed over me. I was still Beth Schulman somewhere. Thank God. I held onto my schedule and the secretary told me to go to my homeroom. Just then, the bell rang. I wasn't sure what to do. The secretary must've sensed my uncertainty because she walked through the little door that swung open in the middle of the counter. She seemed so much taller on the other side. I felt tempted to look behind the counter to see if she'd been standing on a stool.

"This way, dear," she said motioning for me to follow. She pointed down the hall and told me to go directly to my first period English class in Room 6. Room 6 was just a few feet away from the office, so I made it there without a problem. The room was crowded with desks filled with kids. The only empty desk was right in the front of the room. No one seemed to notice me.

I managed to stay invisible for the entire morning. The teachers spent most of each period trying to quiet down the kids and we didn't really do any work, which was fine by me. As I entered the cafeteria, a short chubby girl with cropped black hair, parted in the middle and dotted with dandruff, tapped me on the shoulder. I recognized her from my first period English class.

"Hi, I'm Debbie. Wanna sit with us?" she asked.

"That'd be great," I said, looking around to see who "us" was.

Maybe I would actually make some friends here. We walked past 9 cafeteria tables before Debbie finally stopped and said, "Okay, here's where we sit." A big fat boy sat in the middle of the long table. He sat alone. His face looked sort of flat and his eyes were shaped like almonds. When he saw Debbie he waved his arms and shouted, "Hi Webbie! Hi Webbie! I missed you!"

"Hi Bobby," Debbie said with a big smile, "This is Beth. She just moved here."

Bobby threw his arms around me and my whole body stiffened. A bubble of snot emerged from his left nostril. I backed away.

"Okay Bobby. That's enough," Debbie said, like she was talking to an over-excited puppy.

Debbie told me about her brother, Bobby. He was actually 16-years-old. He attended the special education classes housed in the basement of the Junior High.

"Yo, retard, what's up?" three tough looking guys wearing baseball caps backwards shouted as they walked by our table.

Bobby pounded his fists on the table and the whole thing shook.

"I'm no retard. I'm no retard!" he screamed.

"Shhh." Debbie reached over and rubbed Bobby's arm lovingly. "Just ignore them."

I wondered if sitting with Debbie and her brother had been a big mistake. But then Debbie started asking me about where I used to live and what my old school was like. It felt good to talk about Kew Gardens. I told her about my best friend, Jenny, and the annoying speech therapist at PS 99. I didn't tell Debbie my parents were divorced or that we lived in my mom's boyfriend's house with no running water. Thankfully, Debbie didn't pry. It's as if she knew which questions were safe and which weren't.

When the school day ended and it was time to go home, I felt suffocated by worry. I spent the entire bus ride home terrified I'd miss my stop at Hendrickson Street and Avenue U. I kept my arm stretched up, holding onto the cord above the windows. The cord let out a beep when you pulled it letting the driver know you wanted to stop. My arm ached by the time the bus got to Hendrickson Street and Avenue U, 20 minutes later. I pulled the cord and let out a sigh of relief. For the first time all day, my shoulders relaxed and my stomach wasn't tied in knots.

Chapter 16:
The New Normal

LIVING IN BROOKLYN was far from normal, but by then I'd forgotten what normal felt like. After being there a few weeks, we established some basic routines. Mom woke us at 5 o'clock each morning, just before she and Saul left for their day at the Flea Market. Ellen usually went right back to sleep, but I'd lay there wide awake in our single bed with the sheet separating us. A digital clock sat on top of a cardboard box next to the door and I watched the red numbers click the minutes away until it read 6:00. I'd nudge Ellen and we'd dress in silence. We still had no water, so flushing the toilet became a daily challenge. We'd have to wait till we both used the bathroom before attempting to flush. Then, we'd pour a little bit of water from the bucket Saul got from the neighbors at night into the toilet and pray it would be enough to make the toilet flush. This was our new normal.

During the school week, I continued to stay under the radar. Lots of kids in my classes were really bad, cursing and talking back to the teachers. I kept quiet, sitting at my desk with my head down and the teachers left me alone. They spent all their time yelling at the bad kids. The assignments they gave were easy, compared to the work at P.S. 99. The best part of the school week was coming home and hanging out with Ellen. Mom and Saul wouldn't come home from the Flea Markets till way past dark, so Ellen and I had the house to ourselves most afternoons. We spent our free time watching TV in Saul's living room/bedroom. The TV was a tiny black and white but it was better than nothing. When Saul was home, he was in charge of the TV and everything else in his house. He would constantly remind us that we were living in *his* house now and we needed to abide by *his* rules. It seemed like every day he'd add a new "house" rule. No TV after school; no eating any of "his" food (including all the Twix candy bars he kept in the freezer); no doors closed (that rule followed us from our garden apartment in Queens).

It was Thursday at 3pm when I walked through the door and found Ellen rummaging through the kitchen cabinets for a snack. Except for an opened box of spaghetti and a few cans of stewed tomatoes, they were completely bare. Ellen suggested we throw caution to the wind and go for one of Saul's frozen Twix bars. We opened our bars simultaneously and started to giggle. My head buzzed with excitement. Breaking one of Saul's rules felt exhilarating and dangerous. We hid the wrappers underneath some other trash in the garbage can next to the fridge. Ellen suggested we melt the Twix bars over the gas stove, which seemed like a great idea. She turned up the flame and we held our bars over the fire. It reminded me of the time we roasted marshmallows on sticks over the open fire at camp. The candy bars melted fast and we had to eat them quickly before they made a big mess. My fingers were covered with warm chocolate and the sweet candy made me happier than I'd felt in a very long time. We washed our hands and headed into Saul's room to watch TV. Ellen turned on *One Day at a Time*. We got comfortable on Saul's bed and started to watch.

* * *

I don't remember when we fell asleep, but I woke suddenly to the sound of Saul's big truck pulling up in front of the house. CBS Nightly news was just ending and I shook Ellen to wake her up. Without uttering a word we knew exactly what we had to do. Ellen turned off the TV and we raced into the kitchen, grabbed our book bags and threw a few textbooks on the table. When the front door opened, my heart beat so loud and so fast, I thought it would pop right out of my chest.

"Hey girls," Mom said, "are you doing your homework?

She was carrying several plastic bags filled with loaves of bread. Probably the stuff they didn't sell at the Flea Market.

"Yup," we answered in unison.

Saul stood right behind her. His big belly came through the door before the rest of him entered the room. He wore his usual outfit. Dark blue work pants with a "Dickies" label sewn into the back pocket (how appropriate) and a white t-shirt stained with a day's worth of sweat. He walked into the kitchen and I could see from the glare in his tiny brown eyes he was in a foul mood. I expected him to start yelling at us for not getting up to help Mom with her bags, like he'd done so many times before. But he didn't say a word. He stormed by the kitchen table and walked right passed the trash can where we'd buried the Twix bar wrappers. He'd been known to search the trashcan for proof we'd eaten his stuff, but when he didn't stop I thought we'd dodged a bullet. Within seconds he was back in the kitchen standing in front of us. He grabbed the edge of the table where we sat and it looked like he was trying to keep himself from falling down. His lip twitched and the vein on the side of his head bulged. I knew something bad was about to happen.

"Were you two watching TV?" his voice was measured.

"No."

"Hey Gaye- come in here," Saul yelled for mom.

Mom came right away. No surprise there. She had become Saul's obedient pet.

His voice got louder, "Tell your mother what you just told me?"

"What?" I asked.

"Are you a fucking idiot? What did you just tell me?"

"We weren't watching TV," Ellen chimed in.

Then he grabbed our arms, squeezing tight and pulled us through the kitchen and into his bedroom. Mom followed close behind.

"Gaye, feel the top of the TV," he demanded.

"It's warm," Mom said glaring at us.

"That's right. You *were* watching TV. Do you think you don't need to follow the fucking rules around here? This is my house and you're not getting away with this shit!"

Mom started to bite the corner of her lip. She did this whenever she was nervous or angry. I figured she was nervous *and* angry this time. Nervous about what Saul might do next and angry at us for provoking him. Ellen and I stared at the floor without speaking or looking up.

Saul stormed out of the room and came back with two toothbrushes.

"Now you'll use the bucket of toilet water and scrub the goddamn bathroom floor! Don't even think about stopping until I say so! I want the fucking tile to shine!"

He grabbed my hair and pushed me down. My head just missed hitting the edge of the toilet seat. I got on my knees and started scrubbing the chipped bathroom tile. I secretly wished my head had hit the toilet seat. I wished it had cracked open and bled all over Saul's dirty tile floor. I felt trapped in the middle of a twisted Cinderella story, with no hope of being rescued by a "Prince Charming." No "Happily Ever After" for me.

Chapter 17:
Everything Changes

SAUL SEEMED to come up with a new stupid task for us to do every day after school. God forbid we had any down time to watch his beloved TV. The worst job was weeding his overgrown backyard. The ground was carpeted with knee-high prickly weeds. Not even one blade of grass in sight. The weeds were so high you could barely see the rusted chain-linked fence surrounding the area. My fingers bled trying to pull the weeds out by the roots which Saul insisted was the only way to get rid of them.

Saul didn't just make up stupid rules for us. He and Mom had a bunch of idiotic rules for Dad also. And Dad, in typical Dad fashion, obeyed each one, never once resisting. If even Dad couldn't stand up to Saul and Mom, how could I? He wasn't permitted to pick us up at Saul's house. He had to meet us on the corner of Hendrickson Street and Avenue U. He wasn't permitted to call us on the phone, even though he'd called us every morning since he moved out of our garden apartment. He'd give us the daily weather report, tell us to work hard at school and ended each call with an "I love you." Shortly after moving to Brooklyn I overheard Mom talking to Dad on the phone.

"Our new address is 2163 Hendrickson Street, Brooklyn, NY. Make sure you send the child support to this address from now on," Mom said firmly.

Then she continued in a real snarly tone, "You are not to call the girls on this phone." Dad must've said something about the morning weather calls because Mom said, "Issac, they are big girls! I think they know how to

turn on the radio to get the weather report in the morning!" She ended the
call with, "Get a life!" and then slammed the phone down.
Saul snickered, "Way to put him in his place, Gaye."
I wanted to punch Saul in his big fat stomach.

I thought about how much I missed Dad's morning calls while Ellen
and I sat on the curb waiting for him to arrive. It was a Wednesday
night in November and I watched my breath float from my lips, like
smoke from a chimney. I rubbed my hands together to stay warm. It
was 10 minutes after 5 and I started to feel annoyed. I hated waiting.
Dad had to take two subways and a bus to get to us from his place in
Astoria, Queens, but that didn't stop me from feeling angry.

"Hi girls," Dad waved at us from halfway down the block.

His black overcoat was buttoned tight around his neck and a big
black furry hat with flaps extending over his ears sat on top of his
head. He looked ridiculous. How embarrassing. It's not like I knew
anyone scurrying by us on the street, but I looked around anyway to
see if people were staring.

I'd count down the days until I could see Dad and then as soon
as I saw him, I'd feel let down. It was like I had fantasy dad in my
head, but then real dad showed up every Wednesday and I'd find
myself drowning in a pool of disappointment. The disappointment
was always followed by guilt, since I knew it wasn't easy for him to
travel all the way to Brooklyn to see us for an hour every Wednesday
night. Disappointment.Guilt.Disappointment.Guilt.

I got up from the curb and let Dad hug me for a second before I
pulled away. We walked to the Forge Diner across the street, same as
every other Wednesday since we'd moved to Brooklyn. While waiting
to be seated, Dad started to talk in an unusually upbeat voice.

"I met a lady. She's real nice. And smart. And pretty."

"That's great, Dad," Ellen said, giving him a pat on the back.

I couldn't think of anything to say. Dad had a girlfriend. Never
had I even considered the possibility of Dad dating. It seemed absurd.

"Her name is Judith. She has an 8-year-old daughter named
Amy. They live in an apartment off of Flatbush Avenue in Queens."

He reached into his back pocket and pulled out his old worn leather wallet. As soon as he cracked it opened, a picture fell out. There, in black and white, staring right at me was Judith and her perfect daughter, Amy. They both wore black fur coats and matching hats. Amy held a shiny black purse in her little hands. If you ask me, an 8-year-old had no business having a purse. They were both smiling brightly, like life was grand and there was never a mother and daughter happier than the two of them.

"Here they are," Dad said proudly.

"Wow, she's pretty and her daughter is real cute," Ellen said.

Why was Ellen making such a fuss? I managed a pathetic, "Yeah, real nice," and remained silent for the rest of the meal. I barely touched my open-faced turkey sandwich. Mom had Saul. Dad had Judith. Where did that leave me?

I pulled on my old purple parka. The zipper broke last winter so I had to use the snaps instead. The arms were too short. The coat felt all wrong. Just like my life. It's like nothing fit anymore. I didn't fit. I walked outside while Dad paid the bill. I couldn't help but feel tossed aside and all alone. A warm tear rolled down my cheek and I reached my hands deep into the pockets of my parka. I felt something soft and pulled out the little piece of fabric attached to the diaper pin Patti had cut from Jenny's blanket. She'd given it to me almost two years ago and I'd completely forgotten about it. I hadn't gotten to say goodbye to Jenny or Patti or any of my other friends from P.S. 99. Did they wonder where I'd gone? Did they miss me? Why did everything have to change?

Chapter 18:
Secrets

ON RARE OCCASIONS, Saul could actually be kind of nice. Like the time he gave me one of his Twix bars from the freezer when Mom and Ellen weren't around. "Our secret" he'd said with a wink. Or when he let me choose an outfit from one of the bags of used clothing stored in the extra bedroom. So, when he asked if I wanted to watch TV with him I wasn't totally surprised. I'd been in the kitchen drying the dinner dishes. Ellen was in our bedroom reading and Mom was out on the front porch smoking a cigarette.

I walked into his room and there he was lying on his bed in just a tight undershirt and yellowed briefs. A few months ago I would've been shocked seeing him wear so little, but since moving into his house in Brooklyn, it seemed like he was always walking around in his underwear. As soon as he and Mom would come home from work, he'd strip down. Like so many other things, I'd just gotten used to it.

"You can change the channel if you want," he said.

This was a rare moment. Saul never let me choose what to watch on TV. I turned the channel until I got to *The Love Boat*. It was just starting.

"Now come on over and sit with me," he said.

Sitting on the bed next to Saul felt kind of strange, but once I started watching I got lost in the episode. During a commercial, Saul suggested I lay down next to him, so he could scratch my back.

There was a time when Mom scratched my back every night when she tucked me in. That's when she and Dad were still married and our life was normal. Mom would say "lift up" and I'd hoist my nightgown up around my neck and lay flat on my belly. She'd start at my shoulders and use her sharp nails to make tracks all the way down to my butt. It felt so good.

"No, thanks," I said.

"Oh, come on. You can still watch your show."

I laid down on my side and Saul laid next to me. We both faced the television. He lifted my shirt and started scratching. Up and down, up and down. It felt good. About half way through the show, he moved closer. So close, in fact, I felt something big and hard rub against me.

Oh, my God, I thought, *He isn't wearing any underwear!* I started to sweat. I didn't know what to do. I was frozen. Before I could comprehend what was happening, his hand reached around my stomach and he pulled down my sweatpants, along with my underwear. All of a sudden, his finger was inside of me. It was moving in and out, faster and faster. My head began to buzz. I felt dizzy, lightheaded. I closed my eyes tight. When I opened them, I noticed Mom, a silhouette in the darkened room, sitting on the hard chair next to the TV. The only light in the room, other than the TV screen, came from the end of her cigarette.

When had she gotten there? Did she know what Saul was doing to me? She was staring off into space, like she was in some sort of trance. I thought about calling out to her, screaming, "Mom, make him stop!" but I didn't dare. I knew her loyalty was with Saul. Not me. I just stayed there, still and silent, until he was done.

This scene played out at least once a week, for several months. It was as if I was Saul's robot. He'd invite me in to watch television and I would just go. I never said no. It was like another chore. Like washing the dinner dishes or doing the laundry. I didn't tell anyone what was happening. Not my father when he took us to dinner on Wednesdays. Not even Ellen. I knew what Saul was doing to me was wrong, but I felt like somehow it was my fault. After all, I never fought back. Mom usually showed up at some point and took her post on the chair next to the television. I learned to join Mom in her trance-like state. I'd crawl into my head and float above my body. It was like I was watching a movie. It wasn't me lying on that bed, next to a fat old man. It was someone else's life.

Chapter 19:
Flying Bread

ONE MINUTE Saul would be asking me to watch TV with him and the next minute he'd be screaming at me. This Saturday morning was no different. The sun had barely peeked over the horizon when Saul started to shout.

"Hurry the fuck up, Beth. Don't just stand there like an idiot! How many times do I have to tell you, pick up the goddamn boxes and move your ass?"

Before I could respond, Saul slung the metal table horse at me. The sharp edge grazed my knee and as soon as I saw the blood, the tears came hard and fast.

"There she goes again, Gaye. Your little crybaby! That thing didn't even touch you, Beth! Now get up and move!"

Mom didn't even look up. She kept loading boxes on the back of the truck, shaking her head, clearly disgusted with me. I could've been bleeding to death and she wouldn't have cared. Ellen dropped the box she'd been holding and ran towards me. She pulled a tissue from her sweatshirt pocket and pressed it against my knee to stop the bleeding.

"Ellen, leave the goddamn baby alone and get to work," Saul's voice was so loud I thought he'd wake the whole neighborhood.

I stood and shoved the blood-stained tissue into the pocket of my jean shorts. I limped over to a box, picked it up and carried it to the truck. I looked down at my knee. The bleeding had stopped. I probably wouldn't even have a scar. My heart sunk. Why couldn't he just break my arm or fracture my leg. At least then everyone could see how much he hurt me. All the hurt Saul inflicted – when he called me stupid and when he told me I caused Mom's multiple sclerosis and when he touched me in places he shouldn't – all those scars were buried deep inside me.

We finished loading the truck and Saul told us to hurry up and get in. Since we were selling baked goods, our first stop was to Mrs. Smith's bakery warehouse. Saul pulled the truck around to the back of the long building and parked beside three big metal dumpsters. I looked out the window of the truck and saw two rats chasing each other up the side of the first dumpster. Yuck. The rats reminded me of the mice we used to have in the kitchen at our garden apartment. Those things used to terrify me. Now that we were stuck in Brooklyn, I'd do anything to go back to my kitchen room in Queens. Mice and all.

Saul climbed up the dumpster next to the rats. My stomach churned as I watched him pull out whole pies, still in their boxes, from the dumpster. He was just like those filthy rats stealing whatever he could get his hands on. He called to Mom who remained in the front seat smoking her cigarette, oblivious to the whole thing. He told her to load the pie boxes into the back of the truck. She put out her cigarette in the truck's ashtray and did as she was told. He pulled out a dozen, two dozen, too many to count. I wondered if Saul could go to jail for stealing those pies. I prayed for a policeman to pull up and arrest him.

We drove away from the building and a few minutes later we were sitting in front of a Dunkin Donuts. Saul strutted in like he owned the place, while Ellen, Mom and I waited in the truck. A few minutes later, he walked out of the store pushing a rack of day-old donuts. A man in a white apron followed him. Saul loaded the donuts into the truck and took a wad of bills from his pocket. He handed a few of the bills to the man in the apron.

He told us we weren't allowed to tell the customers the donuts were from Dunkin Donuts. More lies. More secrets. I felt like an accomplice. If a policeman stopped us, maybe we'd all be arrested. Our final stop was at the Wonder Bread factory. Saul went into the factory and came out carrying several trays of bread. He bragged about how he got the bread for half price, since it was already expired.

When we finally got to the Flea Market, Saul told Ellen and me to sit in the back of the truck and inspect the pies. If we saw any mold on top, we were to scrape it off with a plastic knife. We were forced to do Saul's dirty work. Knowing we were tricking people made my chest tight and my stomach ache.

It was a slow day at the Flea Market and unusually warm for the beginning of April. The lemon meringue, blueberry and Dutch apple pies were stacked high on the table. The plastic box tops were wet with moisture. The donuts were melting in the hot sun and the loaves of bread looked pathetic. It was already 10 in the morning and we hadn't sold one thing.

Saul began to pace back and forth in front of our table, hands behind his back, looking like a wild dog.

He grabbed a loaf of bread from the table, waved it above his head and yelled, "Day-old bread for sale, get your day-old bread!"

A few people walked by without stopping.

His voice got louder and angrier, "Free bread over here! Come get your free bread!"

No one even looked over at him. The vein next to Saul's beady eyes started to bulge and I knew something really bad was about to happen. My palms started to sweat and I pushed my hands deep down into the pockets of my apron. Saul grabbed a loaf of bread from the table, squeezed it between his thick fingers and threw it at a young woman walking by.

"Ouch!" she cried. "Where did that come from?"

A crowd gathered around our table.

Saul had an audience now and he continued his rant, "Free fucking bread you assholes. Come get your free fucking bread!"

I wanted to crawl into a hole, evaporate into the air or go up in flames, anything but stand there and witness Saul's public rage. People stared and whispered. I looked to see if there were any security guards around. I prayed for a big strong man in uniform to slam Saul up against the truck, cuff him and cart him off to jail. I wanted him gone. Forever.

Finally, one of the produce guys came over, grabbed Saul's arm and said, "Chill, man, chill." Saul stopped yelling and looked over at Mom who was biting the side of her lip anxiously.

"Let's get the hell out of here, Gaye."

It was just after 11 in the morning and there we were loading the truck to go home. I should've been relieved, since we never got to leave early, but all I felt was ashamed and embarrassed.

Chapter 20:
Secrets Revealed

THE NEXT DAY was Sunday, but Mom didn't wake us early to go to the Flea Market. When I opened my eyes, the red numbers on the digital clock read 9 o'clock. Mom stood in the doorway of our bedroom with her hands on her hips. I wondered if she'd been standing there long. She wore a loose-fitting peach nylon nightgown.

She walked over to the single bed Ellen and I shared and whispered, "I let you sleep in this morning. We're not working at the Flea Market today. Saul is under a lot of stress and needs a day off."

We hadn't had a Sunday off since we moved to Brooklyn 8 months earlier. Mom said she and Saul were going to spend the day together. Alone. They didn't say where they were going or when they'd be back, but it didn't matter. Ellen and I had the house to ourselves and we didn't have to work at the Flea Market. We spent most of the day in our pajamas watching TV. In the late afternoon, Ellen said she was going to take a shower and I followed her into the bathroom to keep her company. I lowered the lid of the toilet seat and sat down. Since moving to Brooklyn, we always kept each other company in the bathroom.

I said, "It's weird to think that just a few months ago we didn't even have water or electricity in this place."

"I know," Ellen said, tossing her nightgown to the floor and turning on the water in the shower. "But you know what? With or without water or electricity, this shithole will never feel like our home."

"That's for sure."

Ellen stepped into the shower and closed the mildew-stained curtain. She was quiet for a minute, but then began to talk slowly. "Betty, umm, does Saul ever touch you?"

"What do you mean?" I asked feeling a little nauseous. I knew exactly what she meant.

"Umm, like does he ever touch you...down there?"

I nodded slowly. Then, realizing Ellen couldn't see me from behind the shower curtain I whispered, "Yes."

The water stopped running and the bathroom became real quiet. I stood and glanced into the mirror above the sink. It was all steamed up and my face looked fuzzy. I slowly pulled the shower curtain open and Ellen sat in the tub naked with her arms wrapped around her bent legs, holding them close to her chest, her head buried in her knees. Her long, thick hair, hung sopping wet around her legs. I stood there, not knowing what to say or do. Ellen looked so small all curled up like that. She started to cry. She sobbed and sobbed. Her whole body shook.

"It's okay," I said, reaching out to touch her wet hair. None of this was okay, but seeing Ellen so upset made me feel helpless and jumpy. Ellen finally lifted her head. Her face was red and blotchy.

"He promised if I let him do it to me, he wouldn't touch you. He's such a goddamn liar!" she shouted.

She was trying to protect me and I didn't even know. Tears streamed down my cheeks.

Ellen stood and dried off slowly. She put her nightgown back on and gave me a big, long hug and kept saying, "I'm so sorry, I'm so sorry."

"It's okay," I said, again at a loss for words.

We stood there hugging for a long time.

She whispered into my shoulder, "I really hate him, Betty. I couldn't even protect you. I can't be here anymore."

I hugged her tighter.

She said it again, "I just can't be here anymore."

I wasn't sure what to say, so I suggested we take a nap. She nodded and followed me into our bedroom. Ellen didn't make me put the sheet between us. I curled up close to her and we drifted off to sleep holding hands.

When I woke up, the numbers on the digital clock said 8 pm. We'd been asleep for 4 hours. I rolled over carefully, not wanting to disturb Ellen. I laid there on my back, staring up at the peeling paint on the ceiling. It reminded me of the way your skin peels after a sunburn. I had that kind of burn last summer at camp. It hurt real badly at first, but after a few days, my skin went from bright red to only a little pink. Then my skin started to peel. It was fun peeling the dead skin away, like peeling off dried-on glue.

I wished I were back at camp, far away from Saul and Mom. My head hurt and I closed my eyes hoping to ease the pain. Ellen's desperate voice echoed in my brain, "I can't be here anymore, I can't be here anymore." I rubbed my palms against my forehead, trying to erase her voice, trying to erase the pain. But it was no use. I couldn't get those words out of my head.

I got up and tiptoed into the kitchen, stopping at the freezer to grab one of Saul's Twix bars on my way to the table. I ripped the package open and bit into the frozen layers of chocolate, caramel and cookie. It was so hard, I could've chipped a tooth, but I didn't care. Fuck Saul and his precious candy. I bit off big chunks. My jaw ached from chewing it, but I wouldn't stop.

What did Ellen mean when she said, "I can't be here anymore?" Was she planning on running away? Where would she go? Having Ellen there was the only thing that made it all bearable. I couldn't go on living there without her.

The lights from Saul's truck filled the dimly-lit kitchen. I peeked out the window and saw Mom and Saul walking up the front steps. I quickly buried the empty Twix wrapper in the trash can.

As soon as Mom opened the door she said, "What's wrong with you? You look like the cat that ate the canary?"

"I'm worried about Ellen," I blurted out. And then, like a loose cannon, I shouted, "I think she's going to run away!"

I started to cry. Saul shook his head and stared at me with his beady brown eyes.

"Let her go. I'd like to see her survive out there on her own. She doesn't realize how good she's got it here."

Mom said nothing. She just sat down, elbows on the kitchen table, head in her hands.

"Stop upsetting your mother and get to bed," Saul said through clenched teeth and motioned for me to leave the room.

Chapter 21:
The Truth

A WEEK LATER, Mom told us we were going to see a counselor so Ellen could talk about her problems. Ellen glared at me. I hadn't told her what I'd said to Mom and Saul because I was afraid she'd be mad at me. And I was right. She *was* mad. Really mad. We pulled into the parking lot of a three-story brick office building. We entered the building and took the elevator to the second floor. We got to a door with a sign that said Jewish Family Services posted above it. The waiting room had no pictures hanging from the white walls, no people sitting in the metal chairs lined up around the room. A low rectangular table with a glass top sat in the middle of the room with magazines scattered on top.

Ellen grabbed a magazine from the table and sat on one of the metal chairs. I sat next to her. Mom and Saul sat on the other side of the room. Mom held her red vinyl purse close to her chest as if someone was going to snatch it. Saul flipped through a magazine, while grinding his teeth.

"Want to play Name that Tune," I asked Ellen.

"No!"

"I'm sorry for telling. Please don't be mad."

Ellen ignored me and continued to read her magazine.

A tall woman with brown hair, short, but stylish, wearing a tailored skirt and silky blouse walked through the office door. She introduced herself. Her name was Mrs. Pearlstein. She asked Ellen to come with her. I picked up a *Highlights* magazine and fingered through the pages. I felt too nervous to read, so I just looked at the pictures. I'd peek up from the magazine periodically to look at Saul and Mom sitting across from me. Saul's arms were folded tight against his big belly and his lips were pressed together. The veins beside his eyes bulged, like his head might explode at any moment. Mom hadn't loosened her grip on the red, vinyl purse. She continued to bite her lip and tap her foot nervously. I put the *Highlights* magazine back on the table and picked up a word search. I didn't have a pencil so I used my finger to make an imaginary line around the words I found. The waiting room didn't have a clock, but it seemed like Ellen had been gone for a long time.

Finally the door to Mrs. Pearlstein's office opened and Mom, Saul and I all looked up at the same time. Ellen stood beside Mrs. Pearlstein, her eyes bloodshot and swollen, her nose red and drippy. Mrs. Pearlstein gave Ellen a box of tissues and told her to take a seat.

"It's your turn," Mrs. Pearlstein's voice, smooth as honey, surprised me.

"My turn?" I asked confused. I thought we were there for Ellen. I tried to make eye contact with Ellen, but her eyes remained glued to the floor.

"Go on, Betty," Mom said in her high-pitched sing-song voice. Her fake concerned voice. The voice I'd come to despise. My heart started to beat real fast.

I followed Mrs. Pearlstein into her office. Two high-backed overstuffed chairs sat in front of a shiny wooden desk. A neat pile of manila folders were stacked on top. I carefully eased myself into one of the chairs and my feet didn't even touch the ground.

Mrs. Pearlstein sat in the chair beside me and said, "Please don't worry, Beth. You're not in trouble. I promise. I'm here to help."

I nodded.

"Tell me what it's like for you at home," Mrs. Pearlstein said.

"Ummm, it's okay."

"Ellen told me you have lots of chores and your weekends are spent working with your mother and Saul at the Flea Markets."

"Uh, huh."

"Tell me what a typical day is like for you at home."

I started to talk about all the rules and the stupid chores and the long days at the Flea Market.

"Sounds like a lot of responsibilities for two young girls."
I nodded and my eyes began to tear.

Mrs. Pearlstein leaned in a little closer to me and asked, "Does Saul ever do anything that makes you feel uncomfortable?"

"Well, he yells a lot. He can be really mean sometimes. He tells me I'm stupid and slow and calls me an idiot."

"Uh, huh. How does that make you feel?"

"Awful. I miss my old house and my friends. I miss Patti, Jenny's mom. She was always so nice to me." My voice started to shake. I bit my lip fighting hard to hold back the tears.

"Has Saul ever touched you in a way that makes you feel uncomfortable?" Mrs. Pearlstein continued in an even tone.

I knew I should tell her about how Saul asked me to lay with him, so I can watch TV. How he scratched my back and it felt good at first. But I was ashamed and embarrassed and I couldn't even look at Mrs. Pearlstein. If Saul knew I told Mrs. Pearlstein about the stuff he did to me, he'd be furious. Maybe she'd think it was my fault anyway, since I never told him to stop.

"You can tell me anything. You are safe here," Mrs. Pearlstein said, as if she were reading my mind.

I began slowly, "Saul sometimes does stuff to me."

"What kinds of stuff, Beth?"

"He touches me down there. But, I don't tell him to stop and sometimes it feels kind of good and I guess it's not really his fault."

Before I knew what was happening, tears streamed down my face. I couldn't stop myself from crying. Mrs. Pearlstein took both my hands and held them in hers. Her nails were perfectly manicured and her palms felt soft. She held my hands tight and we sat like that for what seemed like several minutes, hours, days, maybe. She smelled like butterscotch candy.

When she spoke, her voice was smooth and gentle. "Listen carefully, Beth. What Saul did to you is wrong. He is a grown-up and you are a child. Grown-ups are supposed to keep children safe. What he did to you is not something a child should have done to them. The fact it felt good is a physical reaction. It does not mean it's your fault. You didn't ask for it or encourage it in any way. This is *not* your fault. Do you understand, Beth?"

I nodded slowly.

"You and Ellen could press charges. That means you'd go to a judge and testify…"

Before she finished the sentence, I shook my head. "No way, I can't do that."

I once saw an afterschool special on TV about a brother and sister whose parents were drunk all the time. The police came and took the kids away and put the brother in one foster home and the sister in another. What if the judge took me and Ellen away and put us in separate homes? I couldn't live without my sister.

Mrs. Pearlstein handed me a small white card with her name and phone number printed on it in raised letters. I took the card and rubbed my fingers over her name.

"If Saul ever touches you again, I want you to call me right away. Promise?"

"Yes. I promise."

Mrs. Pearlstein stood up and told me to stay there. She left the office and a minute later came back with Ellen, Saul and Mom. She looked directly at Saul and her voice was strong and firm.

"Saul what you've been doing to Ellen and Beth is considered sexual abuse. You could be put away for a long time for what you've done. I've given the girls my phone number. If you lay a finger on either of them again they will call me and I will make sure you are convicted and sent to jail. Am I clear?"

This was the first time anyone has ever stood up to Saul. I wanted to smile, cheer, do a back flip, but instead I stayed quiet and still.

"I never hurt them…."his voice trailed off.

In the elevator going down, I saw that vein on the side of Saul's head throbbing. His lips pressed together tight in a single line, an angry stare in his beady eyes. No one talked in the elevator, but Ellen reached for my hand and that's when I knew she wasn't mad at me anymore.

*   *   *

The remainder of May and June dragged on. Saul and Mom didn't make us go to the Flea Market anymore. When Saul was home, he wouldn't even look at us. His angry silence filled the space. But I didn't care. He hadn't touched me since our visit to Mrs. Pearlstein. I'd always be grateful to Mrs. Pearlstein for being the one to make Saul stop his abuse.

Our classrooms at school were hot and everyone was rowdy, itching for summer vacation. Debbie and I still sat together at lunch every day. She was my only friend. Actually, I couldn't even call Debbie a *true* friend, since she knew so little about me. Well, not the "real" me anyway. I made up stories about my family, afraid if she knew the real story, she wouldn't want to sit with me at lunch anymore. Debbie had to take care of her brother, Bobby, after school, so it wasn't like I could go to her house. And I'd never, ever, ask her to come over to Saul's house on Hendrickson Street. I felt embarrassed by everything in that place. The peeling paint on the ceiling, the bed in the living room, the extra room piled high with overstuffed boxes. All of it. The only thing that got me through the final months of school was thinking about going away to camp. Summer couldn't come fast enough.

Chapter 22:
The Last Summer At Camp

THE BUS rolled into camp at 10 in the morning. When I stepped onto the gravel, the sun shone bright and the air felt crisp. My bunk was in the DEBS Division of camp. That's where all the girls entering 7th through 9th grade stayed. Since Ellen was 15, she could be a C.I.T. –counselor in training – or get paid to be a waitress on the Senior Side of camp. The Senior Side was a camp for old people. They'd come for a week at a time and play shuffle board and do water aerobics. Ellen had decided to be a waitress, so she could start saving up for our escape. Since visiting Mrs. Pearlstein's office, Ellen and I talked about running away all the time. It was like Mrs. Pearlstein gave us the courage and strength to escape together. Ellen had calculated how much money we'd need to live on our own. In a few years I'd be old enough to work at camp too. Maybe by then, Ellen and I would have enough money to start a new life away from Mom and Saul.

Our cousin, Brooke, came to our camp for the first time. She and Ellen were the same age, so they lived together in the Waitress Bunk. I'm not sure why Brooke needed to make money, since Uncle Benny and Auntie Esther seemed rich. They gave Brooke whatever she wanted. Last year when we visited for Passover, Brooke showed us the front flips and back bends she'd learned in her gymnastics class. She also took piano lessons and tap dancing lessons. If you ask me, she was spoiled. And mean. When we visited her for the holidays, she wanted Ellen all to herself. She'd never include me in anything. When I'd ask to join them she'd call me a *tag-a-long* and when I told

Auntie Esther she wasn't being nice she'd tell me to stop being a *tattle-tale*. At camp I had my own friends so I didn't care that Ellen and Brooke spent all their time together.

About a week before Visiting Day, Brooke stopped me when I was walking back to my bunk from the pool.

"Hey Beth, wait up," she called.

I stopped and waited, wondering why Brooke would want to talk to *me*.

She jogged toward me and her thigh muscles bulged.

"How's everything going?" she asked, tucking her straight dirty-blonde hair behind her ears.

"Fine."

"I just got a letter from my mom and dad. They're coming for Visiting Day. They want to take me, you and Ellen, out to lunch."

"Cool," I said nonchalantly, but butterflies danced happily in my belly.

Auntie Esther and Uncle Benny drove to camp in their little tan Dodge Omni. Ellen, Brooke and I waited for them in the gravel parking lot. When they got out of the car, they both looked tired. Auntie Esther pushed back some loose hair that'd fallen toward her face and rubbed her hands over the wrinkles in her khaki skirt. Uncle Benny stretched his arms toward the sky and adjusted his glasses.

I hugged Auntie Esther first and then gave Uncle Benny a big hug, too.

"I'm so happy you came."

"Well, we're delighted to be here, Betty," Auntie Esther said.

She pulled out a shopping bag from the back seat and took out three packages of Oreos, one for each of us.

"Wow, thanks a lot."

We walked around camp. I showed them my bunk and they marveled over everything.

"Betty, you sure do keep your cubbies nice and neat," Uncle Benny said.

"Could you teach Brooke how to be so tidy? I can't even open the door to her bedroom, she's got so much stuff on the floor."

I beamed and Brooke rolled her eyes.

After we checked out Ellen and Brooke's bunk, Auntie Esther and Uncle Benny took us outside and asked Brooke to give us some privacy. She shrugged and went back into her bunk. We sat at the picnic table and my heart started to race. Why would they need to talk with us by ourselves? Was something wrong with Dad? Was Mom sick?

"Girls, we wanted to talk to you about something Brooke told us," Auntie Esther began.

Ellen had told Brooke how horrible it was living in Brooklyn with Mom and Saul. Brooke wrote a letter home, telling her parents the whole story.

"It sounds like the conditions you're living in are awful and we can't believe you have to work in the Flea Market every weekend. We're so sorry you've been living like this. We had no idea."

I wondered if they knew about the stuff Saul used to do to us. I hoped not. I didn't want Auntie Esther and Uncle Benny to see us like that.

"Why didn't you tell your father about all this?" Auntie Esther asked.

Ellen said, "We knew he couldn't do anything to help us and we didn't want him to worry."

"Oh, you poor girls. Uncle Benny and I want to help. Would you girls like to live with us in State College? Now that Ross is in college, we have an extra bedroom that you can share and..."

Before Auntie Esther could finish, Ellen and I interrupted with a resounding, "YES!" and wrapped our arms around her.

Chapter 23:
The Plan

WHEN THE BUS pulled onto the windy road leaving camp behind, Ellen and I could barely contain ourselves. We'd never been so happy to return home. Knowing that Brooklyn wasn't going to be our home much longer made us giddy. I craned my neck and peered around my seat.

Ellen's friend, Michael, sat on the back bench seat, thin, hairy legs sprawled in front of him, bare feet crossed at the ankle and black on the bottom from a summer without shoes. A red bandana covered the top of his head, revealing strings of long shiny blond hair. He strummed a guitar, the muscles on his arms flexing with every chord. Girls in cut-off jeans, straight hair parted in the middle and feathers flowing from their ears, surrounded him. He sang in a quiet, raspy, Neil Young voice. All the kids on the bus were quiet, as if they'd fallen under the spell of the music. Even the bus driver, a jolly looking guy with white hair and chubby cheeks hummed along.

I gazed past the driver and stared at the wide open road. Big old evergreens surrounded us on all sides. Patches of brown grass, looking more like hay than grass, peeked through the breaks in the trees. Beads of sweat dripped down the back of my neck. I took a neon orange nylon band from my wrist and bound up my thick tangled hair. I bent my head, ear to shoulder on one side and then on the other. I straightened my back, butt and chest out, until I heard a crack.

"Ah, that's better," I said.

I turned towards Ellen and said, "Do you think Auntie Esther and Uncle Benny are rich? They live in that big house with the porch out front and that huge backyard. It would be amazing to live there. We wouldn't even have to take a city bus to school, we could just walk."

When I stopped talking for a minute to take a breath, Ellen grabbed my arm and shook me, as if waking me from a dream. "Come on Betty, stay focused. We need to make sure we know what we're going to say to them when we get home."

Ellen cleared her throat like she was getting ready to recite a poem she'd memorized for school, but instead she started to recite the speech she'd been practicing since we left camp.

"I know we've been a burden to you and times are tough, with money and all. It would probably... no definitely... be easier for you to work at the Flea Markets if you didn't have to worry about us. We love you and appreciate you."

"Wait a minute," I interrupted, my voice getting louder, "I don't love them!"

Ellen spoke in a hushed tone, trying to calm me down, as if I were a toddler in the midst of a tantrum.

"Betty, we need to butter them up, so they'll let us go. Just let me do all the talking."

My eyes darted around the bus to make sure no one was listening. I didn't want to blow our cover. At camp, we were just two normal girls from New York enjoying a summer away from the city. I couldn't imagine what people would think if they knew the truth. I lowered my voice.

"Okay, okay, keep going." I waved my hands, gesturing for her to continue and rested my head on her shoulder.

Ellen said, "We'd write letters and let you know how things are going. We could talk on the phone every week. We'd visit."

I rolled my eyes. If we got to live in Pennsylvania with Auntie Esther and Uncle Benny, there'd be no way I'd ever go back to visit Mom and Saul in Brooklyn.

"It's really a win, win. Mom and Saul will have their freedom and so will we."

Ellen nodded in a self-satisfied way.

"Now, Betty, pleaaaase stop leaning on me. It's waaaaay too hot."

"FINE."

I crossed my arms in front of my chest and pursed my full lips. Even though Ellen said please, I could tell she was annoyed and that made me annoyed, too.

The bus driver's hands clutched the steering wheel and he slammed on the brakes. The trees were gone and the highway ahead of us became tight with yellow taxis, city buses and boxy delivery trucks. My stomach did flip flops and I took three gulps, hoping it'd stop. It didn't. I crossed my arms and bent over, willing myself not to throw up. Ellen rubbed my back and I whispered, "Do you really think they'll let us go?"

She put her arm around my shoulders and squeezed.

"This is really happening. We're finally getting away from them."

I wanted to believe her. The lyrics of a Kansas song played in my head, over and over, like a broken record telling me to carry on and promising peace when we were done. The words washed over me like warm water and calmed my nervous stomach. I took a deep breath.

"We will carry on," I said to no one in particular.

Seeing Saul's big white truck waiting in the parking lot of the YMCA gave me that familiar sour feeling in the pit of my stomach. My mind started to race. Will they let us leave? How will we get to State College? Will there be time to say goodbye to Dad?

In the truck, the air felt heavy with our unspoken words. More questions ran through my throbbing head. Did Auntie Esther and Uncle Benny call them? Our aunt and uncle hadn't discussed any of the details when they asked us to live with them. How'd we get there? When would we leave?

When we got to Saul's house on Hendrickson Street he carried our trunks up the flight of concrete steps, one on each shoulder and threw them into our bedroom. He plopped down at his desk, put his glasses on and started shuffling papers, writing checks, looking busy. Mom told us to unpack our trunks and went into the kitchen to start dinner.

When we sat around the table for dinner I moved my spaghetti around the plate, too nervous to eat. Mom never asked about our time at camp. Would she be relieved to get rid of us? My heart ached and I felt surprisingly sad. Ellen got up and started clearing the dishes and I joined her. Maybe staying busy would ward off my sudden sorrow. Mom and Saul left the table and went to sit on the front porch. Ellen washed the dishes and I dried.

"When should we do it?" I whispered.

"Now," Ellen said. She turned off the water and wiped her hands on the dish towel sitting beside the sink.

She grabbed my hand and led me to the front porch.

Saul looked as us with venom in his eyes and spewed, "What do you two want?"

Ellen started. "We know we've been a burden to you. We realize you need a break…"

"Stop right there," Saul interrupted Ellen's well- rehearsed speech.

"Your mother and I have decided we don't want you here anymore. You are ungrateful and selfish and we're done bending over backwards for the two of you. So, pack your bags and be ready to leave tomorrow morning."

My head started to throb and I felt faint.

I looked over at Mom, searching her face for some sign of emotion. She simply sat there on the metal chair, one leg draped over the other, taking long deep drags from her cigarette. She said nothing, just stared into space. That painfully familiar, blank stare.

Chapter 24:
Bye-Bye Brooklyn

WE WOKE to the sound of Saul's fist pounding against our bedroom door before the sun came up. He pushed the door opened and grabbed the one trunk he told us to pack the night before.

"Now get up and get dressed!" he shouted and walked out of our room carrying our trunk stuffed with all our belongings.

Ellen and I quickly put on the same clothes we'd worn the day before. I couldn't brush my hair or my teeth since we'd packed up all of our stuff. I followed Ellen through the kitchen and out to the front porch. Mom and Saul, already on the street, loaded the big white truck and got ready for their day at the Flea Market. Ellen and I stood watching them, not sure what we were supposed to do. When they finished packing the truck, Mom climbed up into the passenger seat of the truck, never once looking up at us. She rolled down her window and I waited for her to say something like, "I love you, girls" or "I will miss you" or even a simple "Goodbye." But instead, she lit the end of a cigarette, took a long deep drag and released the smoke through the open window. Saul marched up the stairs and came towards us. My body got rigid, bracing myself for a punch.

He stuck out his hand and said, "Hand over your house keys."

Ellen and I dug into our pockets and pulled out the keys and placed them in Saul's hand. He folded his fingers around the keys, made a tight fist, turned around and walked down the stairs. He pulled himself into the driver's seat and drove away.

Ellen showed me a little piece of paper Mom had handed her earlier that morning with Dad's address scribbled on it.

"I'll walk up to Avenue U and get a cab to take us to Dad's house. You stay here with our trunk."

I sat down on the big battered trunk and watched Ellen walk down the steps and up the street toward Avenue U. A neighbor walked her little white dog across the street, cars zoomed by and a pigeon perched on the curb, searching for breakfast. My whole life was about to change, but life on Hendrickson Street moved along at its usual pace. The cab pulled around the corner and I saw Ellen sitting in the front seat. It seemed so weird, since neither of us ever rode in the front seat of a car. The driver, a young guy with dark hair and a moustache, got out of the cab and walked up the steps to the front porch.

"Is this coming with you?" the driver asked.

I nodded, unable to speak.

He carried the trunk down the stairs and I followed him. He had no idea our entire lives were packed away in that trunk. He placed our trunk into the trunk of the cab and opened the back door.

"Hop in," he said.

Ellen handed him the piece of paper with my father's address.

When we arrived 40 minutes later at Dad's apartment building, he greeted us in his old ratty plaid robe and slippers. It was just before 7 in the morning. Dad's eyes filled with tears and his coarse hair stood up straight like the bristles of a broom. It looked like he hadn't slept in days. He paid the driver and lifted our trunk out of the cab. He wrapped his skinny arms around us and started to weep. When we got into his one room apartment, we sat on his bed and he explained how he, Mom and Auntie Esther had been on the phone all night making the arrangements. He just kept saying, "I'm sorry, I'm so, so sorry." I hated seeing him cry. I gave him a hug and kissed him on his stubbly cheek. He called for another cab and we all piled in and headed toward Penn Station. By noon, we were on a Greyhound Bus headed west toward our new life in State College, Pennsylvania.

Part Three:
Happy Valley

Chapter 25:
Table Set For Five

"THIS IS YOUR ROOM," Auntie Esther said, with an outstretched arm.

Ellen and I stood behind her in the doorway of our new bedroom.

"It's the biggest room upstairs, so I think you girls will have plenty of space."

The bedroom was triple the size of our room in Brooklyn. There were two single beds with matching pinkish-red comforters. The two windows had pretty cotton curtains covered in yellow daisies. Auntie Esther told us she picked out the fabric for the curtains and sewed them herself. Just for us. Wood paneling covered the walls reminding me of the den at *The Brady Bunch* house. A shiny white desk sat under one of the windows. A white shag area rug covered the hardwood floor between our beds. The sliding doors on the big closet were opened and a few hangers hung from the rod. Otherwise, the closet was completely empty.

"Okay, then," Auntie Esther hesitated. She cleared her throat and it looked like she wasn't sure what to say next.

"It's been a long day for you girls. Why don't you lie down and take a rest. You can unpack later. I'll come get you when dinner is ready."

I walked over to the bed on the far end of the room and plopped down. I stretched my arms above my head and said, "I'll take this one."

"Okay," Ellen said and lay down on the other bed.

After laying in silence for a few minutes, I got up, walked over to Ellen's new bed and crawled beside her. She was on her side and I got on my side. I wrapped my arms around her and we fell asleep.

* * *

A car door slammed outside and startled me. At first I didn't remember where I was and my heart beat fast, fear settling into my belly. I got my bearings and realized I was still lying beside Ellen on top of the reddish pink comforter. Ellen slept next to me. I got out of bed, searching the room for a clock. I figured it must be close to dinnertime. My stomach grumbled. Heavy footsteps raced up the stairs and a second later, Brooke flew through our door.

"Hey, there you two!" she shouted.

Ellen woke up. She clenched her hands into fists and rubbed both her eyes so hard it looked like she'd rub her eyeballs right out of their sockets. This was typical Ellen. Every morning when she woke up, she'd go through this 5 minute eye rubbing ritual.

"Hi Brooke," Ellen said sounding groggy. "Can you believe we're actually here?"

"It's awesome," Brooke said.

I sat next to Ellen and Brooke sat at the end of the bed. She kicked off her white Keds and stretched her legs out on top of the comforter. She wore tight blue jeans and a snug fitting t-shirt. Brooke had virtually no boobs, just like Ellen. I glanced down at my own big boobs and quickly reached for a pillow to cover them up. I held the pillow tight against my chest and felt my shoulders relax.

"I can't wait to introduce you to my friends on the street, Trina and Jody. And of course, my boyfriend, Tommy. That's who just dropped me off. He got this brand new pickup truck for his 16th birthday. We were downtown cruising."

I wondered what it meant to *cruise*, but I decided not to ask. The last thing I wanted to do was look stupid in front of Brooke. Brooke leaned over and gave me and Ellen a big hug. Her long silky blonde hair covered my face and smelled like Marlboro Lights. The same cigarettes Mom always smoked. For the first time, since leaving Brooklyn early that morning, I wondered about Mom. She was probably just packing up from a day at the Flea Market. Was she thinking about us? How would she feel when she got home from the Flea Market and we weren't there? Was she feeling sorry she let us go? I could hear Saul's voice playing in my head, "There you go again, putting another nail in your mother's coffin."

"Dinner time," Auntie Esther's booming voice traveled up the stairs.

Brooke yelled that we'd be down in a minute. She told us to follow her into the bathroom so we could wash up for dinner. The bathroom was right next to our new bedroom. It had a long white counter with a bright blue sink in the middle. Little light blue half-moon shapes covered the surface of the counter. The toilet matched the sink and a dark wood shelf hung above it. A tiny orange towel hung from a rod on the bottom of the shelf. A pretty tan curtain with orange fringe hung in the window. I wondered if Auntie Esther made those curtains, too. The blue bathtub matched the sink and a fancy beige shower curtain hung from a blue rod. The curtain looked like it was made from a tweed material. The only shower curtains I'd ever seen were made of plastic. The bathroom had a warm cozy feel.

After washing our hands, we followed Brooke down the carpeted stairs and into the kitchen. The entire downstairs smelled delicious, like homemade stew or soup, maybe. My stomach rumbled and I said, "Wow that smells great."

Uncle Benny set the kitchen table with five dishes and Auntie Esther stood at the stove. When she turned around, she held the biggest steel pot I'd ever seen. She wore green oven mitts on each hand. A stream of steam floated up from the top of the pot.

"This is your grandmother's famous pot roast recipe cooked in the very same pot she used when your dad and I were kids. I hope you like it."

She then looked at Benny and said, "Please move the Lazy Susan from the center of the table and put the hot plate down. This pot is heavy."

Uncle Benny moved around the kitchen with the speed and agility of a much younger man and had the large ceramic hot plate set up in no time. Auntie Esther placed the big pot on top and then sat down at one end of the table. Brooke sat to her left and Uncle Benny sat across from Auntie Esther. They all had their spots. Ellen and I just stood there, not knowing where to sit.

Auntie Esther said, "Oh, Benny, go get another chair from the dining room."

He was back in a flash and moved the chair across from Brooke over a bit to make room. The dining room chair looked way too big and fancy for the kitchen table.

"Come and sit," Auntie Esther said. "You girls must be starving."

Ellen sat in the big dining room chair and I sat next to her. Uncle Benny asked what we'd like to drink. We both asked for some milk.

"Oh, I'm sorry, we can't have milk with a meat meal. Would you like some fresh apple cider or a cold glass of water instead?" Auntie Esther offered.

No milk with dinner? That seemed like a weird rule.

I'd later learn Auntie Esther and Uncle Benny kept a kosher home for the most part. They never mixed milk and meat or served any pork products or shell fish.

I immediately felt stupid for not knowing their rules, and apologized awkwardly.

"No need to apologize," Auntie Esther and Uncle Benny said in unison.

I inhaled the chunks of tender meat, baby carrots and cubed potatoes. Ellen spent the entire meal moving the meat around from one end of her plate to the other. She nibbled the end of a carrot.

"Is everything okay?" Auntie Esther asked Ellen. "You're not eating much."

"Oh no, here it comes," I thought.

Ellen decided to become a vegetarian back in elementary school. She wrote some big report in 4th grade about the inhumanity of killing animals. Of course, this, like everything else, annoyed Mom and Saul, but they'd given up trying to make her eat meat. I prayed Auntie Esther and Uncle Benny weren't going to get mad.

"I'm a vegetarian," Ellen said.

"Oh, I, umm, didn't realize," Auntie Esther sounded surprised.

"That's cool," Brooke said.

Auntie Esther got up and took a can of chick peas out of the cupboard. She opened them up and poured them into a little bowl.

"I respect your decision to be a vegetarian," she said, "but I will not allow you to become anemic on my watch. She put the bowl of chick peas in front of Ellen.

"Try these," Auntie Esther said.

Ellen ate the entire bowl.

Chapter 26:
School Shopping

AUNTIE ESTHER drove us downtown in the little tan Omni. Brooke sat in the front seat and Ellen and I were knee-to-knee in the backseat. The ride was short, less than 10 minutes.

I didn't know it then, but in State College, everything was just 10 minutes away. I quickly got used to the luxury of small town living. Hopping in a car to go to the store definitely beat relying on public transportation.

We parked in a lot on Beaver Avenue right across from Dank's Department Store. There were just two main streets in State College, Beaver Avenue and College Avenue. College Avenue bordered the campus of Penn State University, where Uncle Benny taught in the English Department. Downtown was packed with bookstores, record stores, clothing stores, jewelry stores, pizzerias, diners and delis.

Auntie Esther held my hand to cross Beaver Avenue and although I knew I was way too old to be holding hands with a grown up, I didn't pull away. Ellen and Brooke raced ahead of us and waited on the corner in front of Dank's Department Store.

"I love this place," I said feeling happier than I'd felt in a long time.

"What place?" Auntie Esther asked.

"This whole town…it's such a happy place."

Auntie Esther laughed and explained that State College was actually called "Happy Valley."

I smiled proudly, feeling like I'd just uncovered a hidden treasure.

Auntie Esther said, "Okay girls, you each get to pick out one outfit and a pair of shoes for the first day of school. Let's start at the shoe department. They're having a Back to School Sale. Buy one, get one free."

"Ellen and I are going to head over to the Juniors Department first," Brooke said.

Before Auntie Esther could respond, Brooke pulled Ellen towards the escalator.

Auntie Esther shook her head and put her hands on her wide hips.

"That Brooke sure does have a mind of her own. See these gray hairs?" She pointed to the loose wisps of hair sticking out of her bun. "They're all from Brooke."

The first pair of shoes Auntie Esther had me try on were called Penny Loafers. She explained how they were the most practical.

"You can wear them with skirts or slacks."

It was funny the way Auntie Esther called pants, slacks. She showed me the part on the top of the shoe, where an actual penny fit. She asked me what color I liked and I pointed to the maroon ones.

"Okay, now I think we better get you a pair of snow boots too. Get ready for lots of snow this winter. We get lots more snow here in State College than you get in New York."

I found a cool pair of boots called Duck Boots. They had thick plastic on the shoe part and the part that came to the knee was made of some comfortable looking quilted material.

"Oh, I like those," Auntie Esther said, "I think I'll get a pair too. After all, they are buy one, get one free."

In the years ahead, I'd learn how Auntie Esther never resisted a bargain.

We both chose the tan ones, since Auntie Esther said they were the most "versatile" color. I didn't know what "versatile" meant but I loved the way it sounded when she said it. I made a mental note to file "slacks" and "versatile" away, hoping someday I'd have a chance to use these sophisticated words.

Chapter 27:
Cigarettes And Candy

I WORE the new outfit Auntie Esther bought me at Dank's Department Store on the first day of 8th grade at the State College Area Intermediate School. I'd showered and laid my clothes out next to my bed the night before. I wanted to make sure I wasn't late for my first day. I walked through the upstairs, past Auntie Esther and Uncle Benny's bedroom door. I peeked through the open door and saw their double bed had already been made. The wooden floor squeaked as I walked across it in my new loafers. Ellen and Brooke were in the bathroom, whispering behind the closed door. I felt a tinge of jealousy creeping up, but I pushed the feeling away and went downstairs. I wasn't going to let anything ruin my first day in my new school. Really, it felt like the first day of my new life.

Uncle Benny sat at the kitchen table drinking a little glass of orange juice and reading a newspaper. Auntie Esther wore an apron and was cooking something at the stove. I stood in the doorway and waited for someone to notice me.

As if reading my mind, Uncle Benny looked up from his newspaper and said, "Wow- look who's up and all ready for school. Good morning, Betty."

"Morning."

He darted up from the table and pulled out a chair for me to sit in, like I was some kind of royalty. I felt like I should curtsey.

"Don't you look pretty today?"

I glanced down at my khaki skirt, light pink turtleneck and mint-green argyle sweater. I did look pretty good.

"Now, what can I get you?" He opened the cabinet underneath the counter. "We've got corn flakes, cheerios, oatmeal..."

Auntie Esther interrupted, "Or I can make you an egg sandwich."

"An egg sandwich sounds great," I said. I wasn't used to someone cooking me breakfast on a school day.

Uncle Benny closed the cabinet door and walked to the fridge.

"What would you like to drink-apple cider, orange juice, milk, water...?"

The fridge overflowed with various drinks and lots of containers filled with leftovers.

"Apple cider, please."

Auntie Esther came to the table and set down an English muffin egg sandwich on a royal blue Fiesta-ware dish.

"I bet you didn't know I was the original creator of the Egg McMuffin, did you? If only I'd sold the rights to McDonald's I'd be a very wealthy woman right now," Auntie Esther said with a wink.

I took a bite and said, "This is way better than a McDonald's Egg McMuffin."

Auntie Esther smiled, leaned over and gave me a kiss on top of my head and said, "Well that's because it's made with love, my dear."

Her kiss reminded me of kisses Daddy used to give before dinner every night. Even though that was 5 years ago, I could feel his lips on the top of my head like it was just yesterday. Just then, Ellen and Brooke charged into the kitchen. Brooke opened the fridge and grabbed a glass bottle filled with milk. She took a big long swig.

"Brooke, if you want some milk, pour it in a cup," Uncle Benny said, sounding annoyed.

"I'm finishing it, so why dirty a glass?" Brooke shrugged.

"Oh Brooke," Auntie Esther said wiping her hands on her apron. "Can I make you girls an egg sandwich?"

"No thanks," Ellen and Brooke answered in one voice.

"We'll just take a bagel to go, since Tommy will be here to pick us up any minute," Brooke said.

Auntie Esther sliced two bagels, spread some cream cheese in the middle of each and wrapped them up in foil.

HONK. HONK.

"That's Tommy," Brooke said. "C'mon Beth, we'll drop you off at the Intermediate School. It's right across the street from State High."

I brought my empty plate to the sink and grabbed my brand new sports sac purse, another purchase from our big shopping day at Dank's Department Store and the first purse I'd ever owned. The purse felt really light since it only held one folder and two sharpened pencils. I felt really grown up, holding my new purse and heading out the door. Until, that is, Auntie Esther gave me a big hug. I wanted to fall apart in her arms. I wanted to cry and hide and sit at the kitchen table with her eating egg sandwiches all day. My hands felt clammy and I started to sweat.

HONK. HONK.

"Let's go, Beth!" Brooke yelled from the front porch.

Auntie Esther seemed to know exactly how I felt. She said I'd do great. She said everyone at school will want to be my friend. I knew she was trying to reassure me, but I didn't believe a word she said. She didn't know how shy I was at school. She didn't know I only made one friend the whole time I lived in Brooklyn.

I reluctantly headed out the door and walked towards Tommy's pickup truck parked beside the little tan Omni in the driveway. Tommy wore a baseball cap and a lit cigarette was propped between his lips.

"Yo." He waved through the open window.

Brooke got in first and Ellen slid next to her.

"Hop in the back, Beth." Brooke said, as if hopping in the bed of a jacked-up pickup truck was something I did every day. People didn't drive pickup trucks in New York City. I'd never seen one, let alone been in one.

"Let me give you a hand." Tommy got out of the truck and made his way over to me.

His baggy Levis accentuated his lanky frame. He bent his leg and positioned his cowboy boot on the truck's fender, grabbed my hand and hoisted me into the back. My wrap-around skirt flew up and I landed flat on my back. Feeling totally embarrassed and clumsy, I quickly straightened my skirt over my knees and sat up.

"Umm, thanks," I managed.

Tommy winked and I noticed his eyes were the exact same shade of green as mine.

It was windy in the back of the truck, so my hair blew every which way. I tried to smooth it down with my hands, but as soon as I stopped, it became one big tangled mess again. The truck pulled up to a Uni-Mart and Tommy, Brooke and Ellen hopped out of the front. "Where are you going?" I shouted after them from the bed of the truck. "Just getting some cigs," Brooke called back and they all disappeared into the store.

I couldn't believe it. Here I was stuck in the back of a pickup truck and I didn't even have a brush to fix my hair. I prayed we wouldn't be late for school. I bet if Auntie Esther and Uncle Benny knew Brooke was buying cigarettes on the way to school, she'd be in big trouble. I imagined myself telling on her as soon as I got home from school, even though I already knew I wouldn't. I didn't want to be called a tattle tale.

"Heads up," Tommy yelled and threw me a bag of M&M's.

I put my hands up, mostly to guard my face, but miraculously caught the bag of candy.

"Now you got something, too, so don't be telling on us."

I immediately ripped the bag open and devoured the candy, even though I wasn't even hungry.

Chapter 28:
Talk New York

"HOW WAS IT?" Auntie Esther asked as soon as I walked through the front door.

"It was great. Really, really great. Everyone was super nice. Even the teachers were kind of cool."

"That's terrific, Betty. I can't wait to hear all about it."

Ellen and Brooke had already made their way downstairs to watch TV. Auntie Esther placed an orange Fiesta-ware plate covered in celery, carrot sticks and slices of red cabbage in front of me. She pulled out a jar of mayonnaise and a bottle of ketchup from the fridge. She put a scoop of mayonnaise into a little glass bowl, added some ketchup and mixed it together into a thick, creamy, pinkish red dip.

"I have Mrs. Cramer for English, she's funny. Ms. Stockbacker for Typing, she's got big hair and long fingernails and I think she's going to be kind of strict. Mrs. Schumer for Music. She looks like a little troll and spent the entire period singing, *Go, Little, Lions, Go, Little Lions, Go, Go, Go!*"

Auntie Esther laughed at my impersonation of Mrs. Schumer.

"Oh, yeah-I can't forget Ms. Rubin. She's my Chemistry teacher and she told us she got hit by lightning. Twice! Isn't that crazy?"

"Wow," Auntie Esther took in every word and seemed genuinely interested.

I dipped a carrot into the creamy mixture and took a big bite before continuing.

"This girl named Sarah is in my typing class and when she asked where I lived and I told her I lived on Smithfield Street, she said we're practically neighbors 'cause she lives on Nimitz Avenue and apparently that's really close...."

"Yes, Nimitz is the street that runs perpendicular to ours."

Perpendicular, I repeated the word slowly in my head trying to figure out what it meant. I'd have to look it up in the Webster's Dictionary I found in the desk drawer in my new bedroom.

"I think her last name is Levick? Her sister is in Brooke's grade."

"Sarah Levick. Yes. That's right. She invited me to walk to school with her and her neighbor, Rebecca."

I was really relieved I wouldn't have to ride in Tommy's truck anymore, but I didn't mention that to Auntie Esther. I used a piece of celery to scoop up a dollop of dip and took a big bite.

"Oh, here's the best part. I met this really funny guy named Jonathan. When he heard me talk, he told me I have a great New York accent. So every time I saw him in the hall, which was like 5 times, he'd say.... Hey, Beth, how's it going? Talk New York. Then I'd say, "Chwocalate" and he'd crack up."

"Oh, Betty, you're a piece of work. Oh, I almost forgot. You got mail today."

Auntie Esther handed me a little envelope with the words BETH SCHULMAN c/o WALDEN written all in capital letters on the front. I recognized Dad's printing right away. I'd never tell anyone, but I was kind of disappointed the letter wasn't from Mom. I ripped open the envelope and found three dollar bills and a letter inside. Dad wrote in all capitals all the time.

9/5/80

DEAR BETH,

I DO HOPE YOUR FIRST DAY IN YOUR NEW SCHOOL IS BETTER THAN YOU ARE EXPECTING. I'M SURE YOU ARE A LITTLE AFRAID, BUT IF YOUR FIRST DAY IS SCARY, YOUR SECOND DAY WILL BE BETTER. I AM ENCLOSING SOME SPENDING MONEY FOR YOU. SO ENJOY.

LOVE, DADDY

I thanked Auntie Esther for the snack and told her I was going upstairs to write back to Dad. She said that was a good idea. When I got to my bedroom, I took the empty shoe box from my Penny Loafers out of my closet. I opened the lid and put Dad's letter inside. I sat at the shiny white desk, pulled a piece of loose leaf paper out of my binder and wrote.

Sept. 8, 1980

Dear Dad,

Thanks for the letter. And thanks for the three dollars. School is much better than I thought it would be. Everyone is nice. We didn't get any homework since it was the first day. Hope you're doing good.

Love, Beth

Chapter 29:
Popularity

THE FIRST FEW weeks of 8th grade flew by. Kids in State College were so different than the kids in Brooklyn. Or maybe it was me who was different. State College felt like camp. I could be myself, without worrying or hiding or keeping secrets.

The students at State College Area Intermediate School seemed to fit into a few different categories. There were the jocks, the geeks and nerds, the druggies, and the hicks. As far as I could tell, the jocks were the most popular and the geeks and nerds were the least. Carolyn Brenner would probably be considered a hick because she lived in a tiny house in the country. She was also a little weird, so some might've considered her a nerd. She was the first person to ask me to sit with her at lunch. I sat with her and a few of her other friends from the FFA Club (Future Farmers of America) for the first two weeks of school. They were all real nice.

Kim and Karen sat near me in typing class. They'd lived in State College all their lives and been best friends since they were in kindergarten. Kim and Karen weren't as friendly as Carolyn. They seemed to be checking me out for the first few weeks of school. Finally, when they heard I was from New York, they started talking to me more. Kim passed me a note at the end of typing class.

It said: *Meet us after school in front of the cafeteria. We have to talk to you. It's important.*
From Kim and Karen

I stuffed the note in my purse and started to worry. Maybe I did something wrong. Maybe they didn't want to be friends with me anymore. I felt sick for the remainder of the day and couldn't wait for it to end.

After school, I headed over to the cafeteria and Kim and Karen were waiting for me.

"What's up guys?" I tried to sound cheerful, praying they didn't hear the fear in my voice.

Kim started, "We've seen you hanging out with Carolyn Brenner. She's a total weirdo and if you want to be popular here, you really can't be friends with people like her."

Karen continued, "We're not being mean or anything, we think you're cool and we just thought we should let you know."

"Thanks for the advice. I totally get it. See you guys tomorrow."

I walked home by myself, needing time to sort through the conversation I had with Kim and Karen. I replayed it over and over in my head. I felt all mixed up. Kim and Karen were just trying to be nice. It was like they were looking out for me, right? It felt all wrong, but by the time I'd gotten home, I'd convinced myself I had no choice. I dialed Carolyn's number.

"Hi," I hesitated for a minute. "It's Beth."

Right away, she could tell something wasn't right. "Are you okay?" she asked.

"Well, I umm, I just don't think I can...Ummm, sit with you at lunch anymore."

As soon as the words came out of my mouth I wanted to take them back. Carolyn's response came as a total surprise.

"I kind of figured this would happen. I've seen you hanging out with Kim and Karen. You're new here and you actually have a chance at being popular. Go for it."

I wasn't sure what to say, so I mumbled, "Okay, well, thanks," and quickly hung up the phone.

Feelings of extreme guilt pulsated through my veins. I knew I'd just done something terrible. But Carolyn seemed to understand which made me feel even worse.

Chapter 30:
The Jewish Community Center - JCC

A COOL BREEZE flowed through our bedroom windows. The daisy curtains looked like they were floating. Even though it was already 10 o'clock on Sunday morning, Ellen and I were still in bed. We'd been awake for awhile, but it felt good to stay under the covers, all nice and cozy. If we were still living in Brooklyn we'd have been at the Flea Markets working for 4 hours already.

I told Ellen about all my classes and how I couldn't believe how many friends I'd made already. I didn't tell her about Carolyn. I felt too ashamed. Ellen hung out mostly with Brooke and her group of friends. She didn't seem to be enjoying school as much as me.

"I'm bored," she said. "I want to get a job and start making money for college."

She'd been talking about college a lot lately. She and Brooke sometimes hung out at the arcade downtown. She'd met some students from Penn State University there.

"I could totally see you at Penn State. And I could see me visiting you on the weekends and staying with you in your dorm," I giggled.

"You'd be welcome anytime, Betty."

I heard the front door open and a second later Uncle Benny called up the stairs, "Bagel time."

"Coming...." I called. I jumped out of bed and since I was only wearing a t-shirt, I pulled on a pair of sweatpants and asked Ellen if she was coming.

"You go on down, I'm going to read for a bit," she said, grabbing her copy of *Catcher in the Rye* from the desk and getting back into bed.

By the time I got to the kitchen, Uncle Benny had placed a basket of sliced bagels in the middle of the table. The whole house smelled like sesame and garlic. Auntie Esther put a platter of lox and tomato slices on the table and opened up a new package of Weis Brand cream cheese. I'd never tasted lox before moving to State College, but it had quickly become my favorite Sunday morning breakfast treat.

"Good morning, dear. Where are the others?" Auntie Esther asked.

"Ellen is reading in bed and I think Brooke is still sleeping. Her door was closed."

Uncle Benny walked into the living room and cranked up Beethoven on the stereo. He came back into the kitchen, waving his arms around, like an orchestra conductor. He looked funny and I started to laugh.

"Benny, don't you think you should turn that down? Brooke is still asleep," Auntie Esther said.

"If Brooke didn't stay up till all hours of the night, she wouldn't have to sleep until noon." Uncle Benny's voice was tight and I thought he might be mad.

I tried to lighten the mood by telling a joke Dad had once told me. "Did you hear the one about the really popular cemetery? People are just dying to get in there."

I broke into fits of laughter before I even got to the punch line.

"Oh, Betty-that's an oldie." Auntie Esther smiled and handed me a glass of orange juice.

"An oldie, but a goodie," Uncle Benny said giving me a thumbs-up.

Auntie Esther said, "I want you and Ellen to take a ride over to the synagogue with me after we eat. I have to drop off the challah I baked for the Bnai Brit Women's luncheon and I really want to introduce you to Rabbi Joel."

"Sure," I said and spread a thick layer of cream cheese on my bagel. I'd never been in a synagogue and I was curious to see what it looked like inside.

* * *

On the way over to the synagogue, Auntie Esther told us about a Sunday School class the synagogue recently started for teens. She also mentioned a group called BBYO which stood for Bnai Brit Youth Organization.

"Maybe you'll want to get involved," Auntie Esther said with a question in her voice.

"There aren't many Jewish families in State College and this might be a good way for you two to meet some new friends."

"I don't think I'll have time," Ellen said. "I really want to get a job on the weekends and after school."

"Oh, well…that's a fine idea, Ellen. I can take you around later to get some applications if you'd like."

"How about you, Betty? Does any of this sound appealing to you?"

"I dunno," I shrugged. "Does Brooke do any of this stuff?"

"Well, umm, no, no she doesn't. Getting Brooke to go to Hebrew School was tough enough. Once she became a Bat Mitzvah at 13, she was done with religion."

An awkward silence crept into the car.

Auntie Esther took a deep breath, breaking the silence. "Well, you know what they say-different strokes for different folks."

She drove into a small parking lot alongside a light-colored brick building. Auntie Esther took the big braided bread from the back of the car and cradled it in her arms like a baby. We followed her up some steps towards the building. Above the double glass doors, the sign said, *Congregation Brit Shalom*, in shiny gold letters.

We entered the synagogue and a chubby guy with rosy cheeks and curly reddish-brown hair greeted us. He wore a little white cap on his head, held in place by two black bobby pins. A fancy white scarf with Hebrew letters stitched along the sides hung around his neck.

"Well, hello Esther," he said in a cheerful voice and leaned over to kiss my aunt on the cheek. "That challah looks beautiful. You've really out done yourself this time."

"Thank you, Rabbi." Auntie Esther was blushing. "I want to introduce you to my nieces from New York. Remember I told you they were coming to live with us?"

"Of course. Hello there." He reached out and shook our hands. His palm felt soft and warm. "It's so nice to finally meet you. I bet State College is a lot different than New York, huh?"

A wave of nausea washed over me and a million questions raced through my mind. What did Auntie Esther tell him about us? How much did he know? Before I could say or do anything, a pretty woman with long black wavy hair walked up to us. She wore a straight black skirt and a silky pink blouse with three pearl buttons at the neckline. Her brown eyes were the size of saucers and her eyelashes looked like spider legs. She wore gold hoop earrings and a thick gold bracelet on her wrist. Rabbi Joel put his arm around her.

"Barbara, meet Esther's nieces from New York. Ellen and Beth, this is my wife, Barbara."

"So happy to meet you," Barbara said and then whispered loudly into Auntie Esther's ear, "It was so very kind of you and Ben to take them in."

Oh, my God. What did she know about us? Her eyes were full of pity. My cheeks got red hot. I felt like some pathetic charity case.

Auntie Esther must've sensed my discomfort because she said, "Rabbi, I was hoping you could show the girls the teen room and tell them a little bit about the program."

"I'd love to, but I have the little tots waiting for me in the sanctuary. They are ready to rock out to some Shabbat Shalom, so I better go. Barbara can show the girls around."

He grabbed a guitar leaning against the window in the hallway and walked away. He called over his shoulder, "It was nice to meet you girls. Hope to see you again soon." He waved and disappeared behind a door.

Auntie Esther put the challah in the synagogue's kitchen and we followed Barbara down some steps. The pointy heels of her fancy black shoes made a clicking sound with every step she took. I hated the way she looked at me and Ellen like we were a couple of dirty little orphans. Her words amplified in my head, *"It was soooooo very kind of you and Ben to take them in.!"* I resisted the urge to stick my foot out in front of her expensive shoes and watch her topple down the stairs.

Chapter 31:
The Makeover

I AGREED to give Sunday School a try which thrilled Auntie Esther. That's where I met Cindy and Liza. We became friends almost immediately. When they told me how much they hated Rabbi Joel's wife, Barbara, I knew we'd be friends forever. They told me stories about how Barbara used to live in Philadelphia, before she married Rabbi Joel. They'd been married for just one year. Cindy and Liza said Barbara thought she was a big deal, being the Rabbi's wife and all. The three of us agreed that Rabbi Joel was way too nice for someone as snobby as Barbara.

"Can you believe how much mascara she wears?" Liza asked.

"And how about all that eye shadow?" I added.

"A *little* make-up is okay," Cindy said, "but Barbara really overdoes it."

The three of us were sprawled out on the cream-colored leather sectional couch in Cindy's finished basement. We walked to her house after Sunday School to play a video game on her Atari. We passed the controller back and forth mesmerized by the bouncing ball on the TV screen. Cindy lived on the same street as Auntie Esther and Uncle Benny, but at the other end. Her house was much bigger and fancier. Her dad was the optometrist in town. Her mom had a big important job at the phone company. Most moms in State College were either homemakers or had part-time jobs, but Cindy's mom was a full-time executive. She dressed in tailored suits every day and wore tennis skirts on the weekends. She even had a full-time housekeeper named Roxy. I used to think Auntie Esther and Uncle Benny were rich, but I now realized by State College standards they were just average. Cindy Levine *was* rich.

"So Beth, why don't *you* wear any makeup?" Cindy asked.

"I don't know," I said, my eyes still fixed on the big screen of her console TV.

"Are you allowed? My parents are so strict, they won't let me even wear a lit bit of makeup. I sneak lip gloss and blush in my purse and put it on at school," Liza said.

"Are your aunt and uncle strict?" Cindy asked.

"Not really..." The way they stared at me, like they were looking for answers, made me feel jumpy.

"I think your eyes would look a lot prettier if you wore a little mascara," Liza said.

Cindy added, "And curling your eyelashes would make a big difference, too."

"I have a great idea, Liza," Cindy talked to Liza like I wasn't even there. "Let's give Beth a makeover."

They hopped off the leather sectional couch and headed up the stairs.

"Come on," they said in unison.

I trailed behind feeling like an awkward ugly duckling.

When we got upstairs to Cindy's room she told me to sit in the chair at her desk. Liza took the round brush sitting on Cindy's desk and started brushing my hair away from my face. It reminded me of the time Penny gave me my first French braid at camp, after gently brushing out my tangled knot. Thank God that knot was long gone.

"So, why do you live with your aunt and uncle anyway?" Cindy asked while applying pink powdery blush to my cheeks.

Liza interrupted, "Cindy, that's rude. Maybe Beth doesn't want to talk about it."

"It's okay," I said. This was the question I'd been dreading.

"My mom is sick, so she couldn't take care of us. My dad lives in a small apartment, so he couldn't take care of us either. So that's why we moved here."

I was impressed with how I condensed my whole messy life into just two simple sentences. In the months ahead, this would become my go-to response whenever anyone asked about my living situation.

Cindy seemed satisfied with my explanation and told me to

close my eyes. I felt a soft swab on my eyelids. It tickled. When I opened my eyes, Cindy came toward me with a metal eyelash curler. It looked like a tiny torture machine. I flinched.

"Stay still," Cindy said impatiently.

I froze and prayed the eye lash curler wouldn't remove all my lashes.

"That's so much better," Cindy said, clearly proud of her handiwork.

"Nice." Liza nodded.

"Now all you need are some bangs to cover up your big forehead."

Cindy's words felt like a kick in the stomach. I'd always been so self-conscious about my big boobs, trying to conceal them with oversized tops, but I never gave much thought to other parts of my body that might be all wrong. I stared in the mirror propped on top of Cindy's desk and my oversized forehead stared back at me.

* * *

The very next day, I asked Auntie Esther if she could take me to get my hair cut. So we drove over to Naomi's Place, the hair salon in the basement of Dank's Department store. Naomi told me to sit in front of the low sink so the shampoo girl could wash my hair. I tilted my head back tentatively. I wondered if the shampoo girl could tell this was my first time in a real hair salon. The shampoo girl asked if the water was okay and I said yes. I felt like jumping up and down and hugging her, telling her how perfect everything was in this salon. The way she massaged my scalp and lathered the shampoo until there were bubbles covering my entire head; the gentle way she combed my hair with her sharp nails; the careful way she shielded my eyes with a cup of her hand while she used the water spray to rinse all the bubbles from my hair; it couldn't have been more perfect.

Naomi, a middle-aged woman with beautiful loose blonde curls flowing down the middle of her back, owned the hair salon. Her crystal blue eyes sparkled and she had a friendly smile. She combed my freshly washed hair and asked how much I'd like to have taken off.

"Just a trim, please," I paused for a moment and then asked if it would be possible to get bangs.

Naomi said, "Anything is possible," and gave me a wink. After she cut my hair, she blew it dry with a big round brush, making it straight and smooth. When I came out to the reception area, Auntie Esther looked up from her PD James mystery and said, "Betty, you look adorable."

On the way home we stopped at McClanahan's Pharmacy to pick up a prescription. I wandered over to the cosmetic aisle, while Auntie Esther talked to the pharmacist. Auntie Esther found me gazing at the eyeshadow and told me to pick out a few things. She even let me get some perfume. I took the lid off of every bottle on the shelf, sniffing each one, before I decided on the Loves Baby Soft body spray.

"Thank you so much," I said as Auntie Esther paid at the register.

On the way home, I held the plastic bag containing my first eyelash curler, eyeliner, eyeshadow, lip gloss and body spray on my lap. I reached up and ran my fingers through my brand new bangs. I felt like a whole new person. And it felt great.

Chapter 32:
A Weekend Retreat

I DIDN'T GET to see Cindy and Liza much at school because we didn't have any classes together. I looked forward to seeing them every week at Sunday School. This weekend we were going to be spending the whole weekend together at Rabbi Joel's retreat center. I'd started to fall in love with Rabbi Joel. Not the way I loved Rod Stewart or Bruce Springsteen. I would've totally married those guys. I loved Rabbi Joel the way Cindy Brady loved Mr. Brady or the way Lori Partridge loved her older, cooler brother, Keith. Rabbi Joel had the retreat center built onto his house way out in the country just for our youth group. That was just the kind of guy he was-totally generous. A stream edged his property and he owned two beautiful horses.

When we arrived we gathered in the main room of the retreat center. It was one large space, with a small kitchen and an open staircase leading to a loft area. There were 12 of us – 7 girls and 5 boys. Most of us were in 8th grade, but there were a few 9th and 10th graders, too. We spent the whole day outside, stream walking, hiking and riding the horses. We picnicked by the stream in the late afternoon.

We got back to the retreat center just as the sun set. I felt completely worn out by the day's activities, but alive and wide awake at the same time. Cindy, Liza and I sat on the overstuffed couch, passing a big barrel of Middlesworth BBQ potato chips back and forth. Rabbi Joel was perched on a wooden stool, strumming his guitar. He wore white painter's pants and a faded grey t-shirt with Coca-Cola printed in red Hebrew letters across the front. His belly popped over the top of his pants, but it wasn't crazy big like Saul's. I tried hard not to think about Saul, but sometimes he just appeared in my head at the most random moments. I pushed the image away as I reached into the Middlesworth BBQ potato chip barrel, grabbing a handful.

Rabbi Joel stopped playing the guitar and told us we were going to play a game. He asked us to sit next to a partner of the same sex. There were an odd number of girls so Cindy, Liza and I got to be together. He told us to think of questions we wanted to ask the opposite sex. He said there were no stupid questions, only the ones that weren't asked. Rabbi Joel would answer the questions from a "Jewish" perspective. He said we shouldn't write our names on the paper, so the questions would be anonymous. Barbara handed out paper and pencils. Cindy, Liza and I huddled together on the couch.

"Let's ask if boys really wake up with an erection every day," Cindy whispered.

She told us her oldest sister read it in a *Cosmo* magazine. This sounded like the funniest thing I'd ever heard and I started to laugh really loud. When Liza saw me laughing uncontrollably she started to laugh, too, and before we knew it, the three of us were in hysterics.

"Okay, giggle-girls, settle down and write your question."

Rabbi Joel had started calling us the giggle-girls, since he said all we did when we were together was laugh. He sometimes threatened to separate us when we were discussing serious stuff in Sunday School, but he never did. We tried to think of something more appropriate to write, but we were at a loss. In a rare moment of Superman-like bravery, I grabbed the pencil out of Liza's hand and scribbled, *Do boys wake up with an erection?* I folded the paper so many times it fit in the palm of my hand. Barbara came around with a brown paper lunch bag to collect our questions and I quickly dropped the tiny piece of folded-up paper into the bag. As soon as I heard the paper plop on top of the other folded questions, I regretted it. My cheeks got hot and my palms started to sweat. I didn't want to humiliate Rabbi Joel. I knew all about humiliation. An image of Saul lying on his bed in only his underwear flashed through my mind. I quickly locked the memory away in the basement of my brain and put three thousand chains on the door, so it wouldn't ever creep out again.

Rabbi Joel held the brown paper bag and shook it up. He reached inside and took out a paper folded too many times. I knew right away it was ours. My heart beat so loud, I felt certain everyone in the room heard it. I stared at the ground and chewed the side of my mouth, just like my mom used to do when she was nervous. I sat between Cindy and Liza and they both elbowed me as Rabbi Joel carefully unfolded our paper. He didn't read it aloud.

He just looked in our direction and with no trace of embarrassment or disapproval said, "Why yes, giggle-girls, the answer is yes."

Without missing a beat, he went on to read and answer the other six questions.

It was at that moment I realized how much I adored Rabbi Joel and how much I wanted him to adore me, too. At our next Sunday School class I decided to ask Rabbi Joel if I could study Torah and become a Bat Mitzvah. I'd seen photos from both Liza and Cindy's Bat Mitzvahs and it looked like they were having a great time. I'd get to spend time learning Hebrew with Rabbi Joel *and* I'd have a big Bat Mitzvah celebration. What could possibly be more perfect than that?

Chapter 33:
Finding My Religion

DAD CALLED US every Sunday night at 7pm. I sat at the kitchen table right by the phone attached to the wall, twirling the stretched-out chord around my finger, feeling impatient. It was only 6:55pm, and I knew he called at exactly 7pm, but I just couldn't wait to tell him the news.

I picked up the phone after the first ring.

"Hi Dad. It's Betty."

"I know who you are," he said chuckling.

"Guess what?" I began but didn't give him a chance to guess.

"I'm going to have a Bat Mitzvah. Rabbi Joel told me he'd help me learn Hebrew and study and even though I'm going to be 14-years-old next month and most kids become Bat Mitzvah at 13, he said it was okay." I paused for a moment, trying to catch my breath.

"Wow. That's big news. You know learning Hebrew is a lot of work. It's not an easy language to learn."

"What are you saying? Do you think I'm too stupid to learn Hebrew?" my enthusiasm had waned and now I was in defense mode.

"No, that's not it, Betty. I just know you don't have any formal training. It's *my* fault. I should've taken you to Hebrew School when you were younger."

I heard his voice crack and I imagined him crying on the other end of the phone.

"This is NOT about you, Dad. Can't you just be happy for me?" My voice was sharp and I knew my words hurt him. I felt bad as soon as they slipped out of my mouth.

"I know you can do it. You're really something special."

His words were muffled and now I knew for sure he was crying. A loud *honk* came through the phone line and I could see him blowing his nose with one of the yellowed handkerchiefs he kept in his back pocket. Why did he have to be so overly emotional about everything?

"Did Rabbi Joel give you a date for your Bat Mitzvah?"

"Yup. It's on June 26, 1982. That gives me a whole year and a half to prepare. I can do this, Dad."

I wasn't sure if I was convincing him or myself, but suddenly having a Bat Mitzvah seemed like the most important thing I'd ever do.

"Hold on a minute and I'll get Ellen so you can talk to her."

I put the receiver down on the table, just as Dad said, "I know you'll make me proud."

* * *

My plans to spend hours alone with Rabbi Joel as he taught me to read Torah were foiled when Mrs. Goldman, a native Israeli and friend of Auntie Esther's volunteered to teach me Hebrew. When I protested and said I wanted to learn from Rabbi Joel, Auntie Esther explained Rabbi Joel was very busy and we couldn't pass up such a kind gesture. So I got stuck meeting with Mrs. Goldman once a week in a little classroom in the basement of the synagogue. She'd drill me on the Alef Bet, the Hebrew alphabet.

Learning to recognize each new character turned out to be much harder than I'd ever imagined. Mrs. Goldman, looked like a prune, little and shriveled. She smelled like the moth balls in Auntie Esther's linen closet. Her bright red lipstick looked all wrong against her pale skin. Her heavy Israeli accent made it nearly impossible to understand a word she said. For such a little lady, she sure could yell. When I mixed up the letters or when I didn't do my homework to her satisfaction, Mrs. Goldman shouted, "Focus, Beth, focus!" But her accent made it sound like, "Fuckus" and all I wanted to do was laugh out loud. Meeting with Mrs. Goldman in the basement of the synagogue reminded me of those dreaded weekly sessions I had with the speech therapist in the closet at PS 99.

* * *

One Sunday after a particularly difficult session with Mrs. Goldman, I got into Auntie Esther's car and slammed the door.

"I'm done."

"What do you mean, dear?"

"I'm not smart enough to learn Hebrew. Mrs. Goldman is mean. I think she hates me. I think I'm too stupid to have a Bat Mitzvah!" Then I started to cry.

Auntie Esther pulled the car over and put it in park. She didn't say a word. We just sat there in silence.

I bit my lip. Was she angry? Did she think I was being a baby? Did she think I was being ungrateful? Did she think she made a big mistake, letting such an ungrateful baby, live in her house?

Finally, Auntie Esther sucked in a huge gulp of air and let out a heavy sigh, breaking the uncomfortable silence.

"Betty, you're a bright and ambitious young lady. You *can* succeed. Mrs. Goldman probably just isn't the right kind of teacher for you. I will call Rabbi Joel and see if he can find someone else at the synagogue to work with you. We will get you the help you need to do this."

And she did. She called Rabbi Joel who decided the best way for me to learn Hebrew was from a cassette tape. I could put it in a Walkman and listen to it over and over again. Rabbi Joel recorded himself singing all the prayers and reciting my Torah and Haftorahportions. Even though I couldn't have Rabbi Joel all to myself, listening to his beautiful voice whenever I wanted was like a dream come true.

Chapter 34:
Halloween Ruined

THE SCHOOL BUZZED with news about the upcoming Halloween Dance. It'd be a costume party and everyone started making plans. Kim, Karen and I decided to go as 3 black cats. I couldn't wait to get home and tell Auntie Esther about my costume. I thought we could drive over to the mall to pick up black tights and a leotard. I also needed black felt and a headband to make the ears and the tail. I ran up the driveway and stormed through the door.

"Hi, I'm home," I called and walked straight back to the kitchen.

Auntie Esther, who usually greeted me with a big hug and a snack, sat in silence at the kitchen table. She wore the same lavender robe she'd been wearing when I'd left for school. Tears filled her bloodshot eyes.

"What's wrong? Are you sick?" I asked. I wrapped my arms around her and gave her a big hug.

Her body trembled, her shoulders collapsed and she sunk further down into the kitchen chair. I tightened my arms around her body and it felt like I was the only thing keeping her from sliding right to the ground. She started to cry. Her hot breathe warmed my neck.

"It's okay," I said trying to calm her. "Everything's going to be okay. Just tell me what's wrong."

Auntie Esther finally pulled herself up in the chair and pointed to a letter sitting on the kitchen table.

I picked it up and recognized Ellen's handwriting.

Dear Auntie Esther and Uncle Benny,

I know you're both very angry with me and Brooke for skipping school. We were wrong and I'm sorry we acted badly. But when you threatened to send me back to live in New York with my mother and Saul, I knew I couldn't stay here anymore. There's no way I will ever go back to live with them. I tried to convince Brooke to stay behind, but she didn't want me leaving by myself, so she came with me. I don't know where we're going exactly, but we'll be careful and we'll call you when we can.

Sincerely,
Ellen

"They ran away?"

Ellen and I had talked about running away from Mom and Saul a lot when we lived in Brooklyn, but why in the world would Ellen want to leave *this* place? We had it so good here. Had Ellen been unhappy? Had I been too caught up with my new social life to notice? I heard Saul's voice screaming in my head, "You're so selfish! You're so selfish!"

I started asking Auntie Esther questions. "Why did they leave? What happened?"

Auntie Esther explained she'd gotten a call from the school counselor last week. Apparently Ellen and Brooke had been skipping school. When she confronted them about it, she threatened to send Ellen back to New York if she didn't start going to school.

Auntie Esther reached for my hand and squeezed tight.

"I'm so sorry, Betty. I would never send her back there. I was just so angry. It slipped out. And now they're both gone. It's all my fault...."

Auntie Esther's words became muffled then because she started to scream. The scream seemed to come all the way from her toes. Was she losing her mind? I didn't know what to do. I just wanted her to stop screaming. If we were in a movie, I'd slap her across the face or pour some cold water over her head to make her stop. But this wasn't a movie. We were in the middle of a real life nightmare.

The next three days were awful. Uncle Benny canceled his classes at Penn State and stayed home. Auntie Esther didn't shower or eat. She stayed in her lavender bathrobe, sitting at the kitchen table, weeping, her head buried in her hands. Uncle Benny couldn't sit still. He paced around the house, made phone calls, tried to comfort Auntie Esther by bringing her tea and crackers, but she refused to eat or drink anything. I was like a ghost, floating around them, going to school and coming home without notice. I didn't tell anyone at school about Brooke and Ellen. I wasn't worried about them. I knew Ellen could take care of herself and I figured she'd call sometime. I was mostly just angry. How could they do this to Auntie Esther and Uncle Benny? How could they do this to me? There was no way I could go to the Halloween Dance now. Auntie Esther was in no shape to take me shopping for my costume and I'd feel terrible leaving them all alone to go to a party.

The phone rang 36 hours after Auntie Esther first found the note. It was Michael, Ellen's 23-year-old boyfriend from camp. Michael reported that Ellen and Brooke spent a night at his apartment in Maryland. He tried to convince them to go back home, but they were determined to keep moving. He said they were hitchhiking south on I-95 going toward Virginia.

Two more tense days passed and the phone rang again. This time it was Brooke. She and Ellen made it all the way to Florida. Auntie Esther started to cry uncontrollably when she heard Brooke's voice. Uncle Benny grabbed the receiver and talked to Brooke in a very steady, serious voice.

"Come home. No questions asked. No punishment. We want to send you money for the plane ticket. We just want you both home."

I sat on the stairs, listening to the whole conversation. My head ready to explode. No questions? No punishment? How could they get away with this?

The plans were made. Ellen and Brooke would be heading home on a nonstop flight from Tampa, Florida. I didn't want to go to the airport to pick them up because I was still mad. When they got home Ellen gave me a big hug and Brooke went upstairs to take a shower.

"Can we please talk?" Ellen asked. The two of us went to our bedroom and closed the door.

"Please forgive me, Betty. I wanted to tell you but I didn't want to make you lie to Auntie Esther and Uncle Benny."

I made her double pinky swear she'd never run again. I told her Auntie Esther promised she'd never ever send us back to Mom and Saul. Ellen went on to tell me about her adventures on the road. She and Brooke changed their names and got all the way to Florida by riding with truckers in big rigs. It didn't take long for me to go from hating her for leaving, to being totally impressed by her courage.

Chapter 35: Support

LIFE GOT BACK to normal after Brooke and Ellen came home. It was as if they'd never been gone. No one ever talked about what happened and it reminded me of all the secrets we had to keep when we lived with Mom and Saul. I wondered if every family had secrets. I knew when I grew up and had a family I'd never make them keep secrets. Secrets sucked. Carrying a head full of secrets was like dragging a heavy suitcase around all the time.

It was mid-November, but it felt more like winter. The trees were bare and the fallen leaves sat in big neat piles on the curb. Cindy called in the morning telling me her mom could drive us to school. I quickly finished my bowl of cereal and kissed Auntie Esther goodbye. I got my coat on, grabbed my book bag and waited by the front door. Mrs. Levine didn't like waiting. As soon as she pulled into the driveway, she beeped and I ran. I hopped in the back of Mrs. Levine's spotless white Lincoln Continental.

I said, "Thanks so much for the ride," as soon as I closed the door.

"Uhhuh," Mrs. Levine muttered, concentrating on applying her lipstick.

Cindy sat in front with her mom and I had the whole back seat to myself. I loved riding in the Levines' Lincoln Continental. I felt a little bit like a celebrity, sprawled out on the black leather seat. Cindy's mom looked very sophisticated, in her tailored navy suit, a string of pearls around her neck. Her hands clutched the wheel from underneath, giving me a good view of her perfectly manicured nails, painted in sensible beige.

I looked down at my nails, short and jagged, and promised myself I'd try to stop biting them. I remembered my mother's nails, usually painted red, long and sharp, except for that one she'd bite all the way down till it bled. It'd only been two and a half months since I'd seen her last, but I'd almost forgotten her voice, her smell. But that one stubby nail, it looked so out of place, I'd never forget it. That's how I always felt in Brooklyn, like I didn't belong there. I felt more at home in State College than I'd ever felt in Brooklyn. I had more friends in State College than I'd ever had in my entire life. In my classes at the Intermediate School, I became known as the funny girl from New York. Just the other day during gym class I made everyone laugh. We'd been playing softball for the first time.

I said, "I don't have an athletic bone in my body. There's no way I'm going to hit that fast moving ball with this hard stick. Remember, I'm from New York. We don't even have grass in New York, let alone baseball fields."

The entire class started to laugh and even Mrs. Reilly the super tough gym teacher cracked a smile.

Mrs. Levine pulled up in front of State College Area Intermediate School and handed Cindy a brown paper bag.

"I packed you a Diet Coke, half a sandwich and some carrot sticks. Do not buy any snacks at the cafeteria today. You really need to start watching your weight."

Cindy grabbed the bag, said goodbye and as soon as she slammed the car door shut, she turned to me and said, "I'd like to shove these carrot sticks right up my mother's ass."

We both started to laugh, but I felt bad for Cindy. She wasn't even fat and her mom was always getting on her about her weight. As we walked into the building, I unzipped my jacket and when I glanced down at my collared button-up shirt, I noticed I wasn't wearing a bra.

"Oh, my God," I squealed and stopped walking.

Cindy turned around and stopped. "What's wrong?"

I pulled her close until her head was right next to mine and whispered, "I forgot to wear a bra today."

Cindy peeked under my coat and saw my floppy, size C boobs pressed right up against my shirt.

"Oh, shit," she said and then started to giggle.

Her laughter was contagious. I giggled, too, and we both stood there in the middle of the hallway laughing our heads off.

The first bell rang.

"Gotta get to homeroom," she said and darted down the hall.

There I was, braless, standing in the now empty hallway of State College Area Intermediate High School. I started to sweat. What should I do? I couldn't take my coat off. Everyone would know. I headed over to the payphone by the front door and called Auntie Esther.

"Hello."

"Hi," I whispered, "it's me, Beth."

"Betty, is that you? I can hardly hear you? Is something wrong?"

"Yeah, I forgot to wear a bra."

"Honey, you have to speak up. What did you forget?"

I raised my voice one decibel and said, "Can you please bring me a bra? I forgot to wear one."

Auntie Esther said she'd need to take a shower and could be at school in about an hour.

"PLEEEEEEASSSSSE, COME NOW!" I shouted into the phone.

"Oh....ok." Auntie Esther sounded flustered.

"Thanks," I said and hurried off to first period.

I sat down in English class, my winter coat still on, when an announcement came over the loudspeaker: "Would Beth Schulman please report to the main office?"

The teacher told me I could go and everyone looked at me with wondering eyes. I got to the main office and there was Auntie Esther holding a big brown paper bag.

"Hi, honey," she said, handing me the bag.

"Thanks," I grabbed it and ran out of the office.

I darted over to the girl's bathroom next to the cafeteria, headed straight for an open stall and put the bra on. I instantly felt better. I stuffed the brown paper bag into the trash can, dumped my coat in my locker and headed back to class. I couldn't wait until lunchtime when I could make the whole story into one big joke. I knew I'd have Kim and Karen laughing their heads off. This wouldn't be the first time I'd tell a joke at my own expense. One trick I'd learned in State College: Make fun of yourself and everyone laughs with you. Making people laugh kept them from asking too many personal questions.

Chapter 36:
Grades

MY WIT GOT SHARPER as the months passed. Every day, I'd see how many people I could make laugh, walking to class, during study hall, in the library. My mind constantly generated material-a clever comeback, a sarcastic response. My popularity ratings were on the rise, but my grades were not. After the first semester of 8th grade I brought home a report card with two Ds and four Cs. I dreaded showing it to Auntie Esther. I didn't want to disappoint her. When she asked to see my report card I burst into tears.

Instead of yelling or getting angry, she simply wiped my tears away and repeated her mantra, "Those teachers just aren't teaching in the way you need to learn."

She hired tutors to help me pass every subject I was failing. Even though she made it sound like it was the teachers fault and not mine, I knew the truth. After all, Ellen and Brooke never needed tutors. I was just no good at school. But I didn't want to let Auntie Esther down, so I worked hard, wrote and rewrote my class notes, never missed a session with my tutors. By the second semester, I'd earned all Cs and Bs. Auntie Esther beamed when she saw my report card.

"See, Betty, I knew you could do it."

I wrote letters to both Mom and Dad telling them how hard I'd been working in school. I also wrote about the money I'd started to earn, babysitting on the weekends. Dad wrote back right away, praising me for my efforts and told me he knew I could achieve great things. Mom didn't write back for several weeks, but when her letter finally came, it was full of details about the Flea Markets, how tired she felt, how Saul's sciatica was acting up. Mom didn't even acknowledge my letter until the last sentence. She wrote, "Glad to hear you're earning some money." That was it.

Chapter 37:
Dead

ON TUESDAY, March 16th the phone rang at 7:05am. I assumed it was Cindy calling to tell me her mom could drive us to school. I raced for the phone, but by the time I got there, Auntie Esther had picked up the extension downstairs.

"Hang up, Betty. I got it." Auntie Esther's voice sounded distant, harsh and cold. I quickly hung up.

A few seconds later, Auntie Esther let out an earth-shaking scream.

I charged downstairs. Auntie Esther stood by the phone, her lavender robe hanging open, revealing her flowered flannel nightgown. A long loud BEEP vibrated through the kitchen. It came from the phone's receiver, which hung limply from the twisted chord. Uncle Benny stood next to her. They both looked frozen, standing there motionless not saying a word. I put the phone back on the receiver to stop the awful beeping noise.

Ellen and Brooke entered the room in a flurry.

"What's going on?" Brooke asked.

"Sit down," Auntie Esther said.

We all sat around the kitchen table.

"Judith called."

Why would Dad's girlfriend be calling?

"Girls..." Auntie Esther put one arm around me and the other around Ellen and pulled us so close, I felt the flannel of her nightgown rub against my cheek.

"Your dad died late last night."

Once the words seeped out of her mouth, she broke down. Tears flowed from her eyes like a water fountain that just wouldn't turn off. Dead? My dad was dead? How could this be happening? He wasn't even sick.

Uncle Benny joined us at the table and explained what happened. My dad had a bad cold. He'd been home sick for a few days. He'd coughed so hard, the lining of his stomach ruptured. Apparently he had some congenital stomach defect that no one knew about. He bled internally. My father bled to death. Judith found him this morning. He was already dead by the time she got there.

I pictured my father lying on his single bed, in his efficiency apartment, his eyes rolled back in his head, guts and blood oozing from a huge gaping hole in his stomach.

Auntie Esther was crying.

Ellen was crying.

Even Brooke was crying.

Not me.

I just sat there at the kitchen table imagining all that blood.

Then I thought I needed to call Cindy to tell her I wouldn't be walking to school. She'd ask why. Should I tell her the truth? How do you tell someone your father just bled to death?

I left the kitchen table and walked up the stairs like a zombie. My zombie fingers dialed Cindy's number.

When she answered the phone, I spoke in a zombie voice.

"Hi Cindy. My dad died. I won't be at school today."

I hung up before Cindy could respond. I stood by the phone, staring into the mirror hanging in the hallway. My skin looked pale, like I'd seen a ghost. The ghost I'd seen was hovering over my dad's bloodied body.

I heard noises, feet on the steps, voices making plans. The hallway became a flurry of activity. I stood in the center of it all, but felt a million miles away.

"Let's go, Betty. We need to pack."

Ellen grabbed my arm and dragged me into our bedroom. We stared into our closet. Ellen's nose was all snotty and her eyes were red and puffy. My eyes were completely dry.

What was wrong with me? Why couldn't I cry? I remembered Mom telling us about the divorce and how I couldn't cry then either? Was I some kind of sociopath?

Auntie Esther came into our room and pulled some things out of our closet.

"It's a shame you don't have any black dresses to wear to the funeral. There's no time to shop. We'll just make do with what you've got."

I wore my first day of school outfit to my dad's funeral. It felt all wrong. Everything felt wrong.

Chapter 38:
Feelings

I SAT IN a cluttered office across from a big fat lady wearing a knitted poncho. Her desk was a mess of papers, coffee mugs and books. The shelves behind her held stacks of books and stuffed file folders piled high. My eyes scanned the titles on the shelf. *What Color is Your Parachute?* and *Tough Love.*

A few weeks after we got back from the funeral, Auntie Esther thought Ellen and I should talk to someone.

"Talk about what?" I'd asked.

So here I sat across from Dr. Messy. The last time I sat in a counselor's office it was a completely different scene. Mrs. Pearlman's office had been neat and tidy. She made me feel safe. She stood up to Saul and saved me from his abuse. But, that was a long time ago and I didn't need to be saved now. What I needed, was to figure out a way to be done with Dr. Messy.

"How are you feeling?" Dr. Messy asked from across the crowded desk.

"Fine, I guess."

"I'm sorry for your loss," she said.

Ever since Dad died, I'd heard, "I'm sorry for your loss," like a thousand times. It was really getting on my nerves. "It's okay," I said.

What was it like being at your father's funeral?"

"I dunno. Weird. I guess. My mother showed up. I wasn't expecting that."

"Hmmmm. How was it seeing your mom there?"

I shrugged. I'd tried hard to put the day of the funeral out of my mind, but it was always there. Like an unwelcome intruder.

My mom and Saul were sitting on a couch in the reception area when we walked into the funeral home. She was wearing a fake fur coat and when she saw me she stood and opened her arms wide. Did she expect me to run over and give her a great big hug? She'd only written me a few letters in the 7 months we'd been in State College.

"It was okay," I said flatly.

"It's alright to miss your mother, Beth."

Dr. Messy didn't have a clue.

"I know," I said trying to move the stupid conversation along.

I stayed stoic for the entire 30-minute session. I'd become a master at hiding my real feelings.

Auntie Esther picked us up from the office.

"So, how did it go?"

"Fine. Everything is fine."

Chapter 39:
The Letter

WHEN I'D GOTTEN the letter from my mom telling me she and Saul had recently returned from a well-deserved vacation in Hawaii, I wondered how they afforded such a big trip.

I went upstairs and took my Penny Loafers shoebox out of the closet. The box contained all the letters I'd gotten from my mom and dad since moving to State College almost one whole year ago. As soon as I opened the lid and saw my name written on the top envelope in dad's neat print my heart started to beat faster. I carefully took the pile of envelopes out of the box and cradled them in my hand. Holding the envelopes my dad had touched made it seem like he was still alive. But he wasn't. He'd been dead for 4 months. I began to sort the envelopes, making a Dad pile and a Mom pile. The grand total was 32 letters from my dad and 10 from my mom. I put the most recent letter from my mom, in the Mom pile and placed them back in the box. I held onto the large stack of letters from my dad. These were the only things I had left of him. I kissed the top envelope and put his letters back in the box and stuck the box back in my closet. That was a month ago and I'd almost forgotten about the last letter from my mom. The letter that described her amazing, well-deserved trip to Hawaii. Until now.

* * *

It was Sunday morning and we'd been out of school for a week.

Sunday School also ended which meant there was no reason for me to get up early. The digital clock on my desk read 7:30am. I heard Auntie Esther and Uncle Benny talking in their bedroom and I couldn't fall back to sleep. I got out of bed and walked toward their room. I knocked on their closed door and in unison, they said, "Come in."

They were under the covers in their double bed, sitting up, pillows propped behind their backs. Their bedside tables were stacked with books, mysteries on Auntie Esther's side and academic stuff on Uncle Benny's. Auntie Esther wore her soft cotton nightgown covered in tiny purple flowers and Uncle Benny wore his blue-striped pajamas. They looked really cute snuggled in like that. I wanted to climb in between them and cuddle up but I knew I was way too old for that.

"You're up early," Uncle Benny said.

I nodded.

"How'd you sleep, dear?" Auntie Esther asked.

"Good," I lied. Ever since the funeral, I couldn't shut my eyes without seeing Dad's bloody body.

Then they looked at each other as if both of them had something important to say, but neither knew how to say it. I got a sinking feeling in the pit of my stomach.

Auntie Esther began, "Uncle Benny and I were just talking about some things we need to share with you about your mother."

My stomach tightened.

"Could you go wake Ellen, so we can talk to both of you?"

"Is something wrong?" I asked.

"We'll talk about it when you get Ellen. Meet us downstairs."

I got back to our bedroom and found Ellen lying on her side with the covers wrapped around her like a cocoon.

"Ellen, Ellen, get up," I nudged her arm lightly.

She let out a snort and rolled over.

"Come on. Get up. Auntie Esther and Uncle Benny need to tell us something."

Ellen didn't move.

"It's about Mom."

This got her attention. She sat up and rubbed her eyes for a good 2 minutes before opening them.

"What's going on?" Ellen asked.

"I don't know. Get up so we can find out."

By the time we got downstairs, Auntie Esther already had the coffee pot brewing. Uncle Benny had poured apple cider into 4 little juice glasses. He handed one to me and and one to Ellen. We sat around the kitchen table. Auntie Esther explained that there'd been money from my father's social security benefits that was supposed to be coming to us. Since we hadn't been receiving the checks, she'd called the Social Security office in New York and discovered the checks had been sent to my mother in Brooklyn.

It all made sense. Our mother used my father's money to take that trip to Hawaii. Heat rose up my neck and my cheeks started to burn. Auntie Esther told us she'd been in contact with our mother about the money. My mother had refused to forward the checks. *That's because she's already spent the money,* I thought. My mother was a liar and a thief.

They'd contacted a lawyer and learned that the only way they could get the money was by obtaining legal custody of us. So, their lawyer sent our mother a letter requesting she give up her legal parental rights so they can become our legal guardians. My mother refused to give up her legal rights. *She didn't want us,* I thought, *she just wanted our money.* Now we had to go to court.

"We need to go to court? Like, are we going to have to testify in front of a whole courtroom," I asked. Images of Perry Mason came to mind.

"Not exactly," Auntie Esther said.

Uncle Benny continued, "Our lawyer instructed us to have both of you write a letter explaining why you want us to be your legal guardians. The judge will read your letters and meet with each of you."

I couldn't believe this was happening. Why couldn't we just have a normal life? What 14-year-old has to go to court? This was so totally unfair. I knew my life is State College was too good to be true.

The next day, we piled into the car and went downtown to meet with Mr. Fred Farley, our lawyer. Mr. Farley was a short man, just a little taller than Uncle Benny. He dressed in a black suit, with a maroon-striped tie. His dark hair parted on the side made him look like a little boy.

Mr. Farley's gentile smile and kind voice made me feel at ease.

As he gave us instructions for writing our letters to the judge, I noticed a framed photograph on his desk. In the picture two little boys played in the sand on a beach. The boys looked exactly like Mr. Farley. He told us to describe why we wanted to stay in State College. We needed to give details about how bad it was when we were living with our mother and Saul. The judge needed to understand why our aunt and uncle should become our legal guardians. We also each needed to write a letter to our mother, so she had in writing our desire to stay in State College. Auntie Esther would make a copy of our letters, so it could be used as a legal document in court.

A legal document? Like evidence? I couldn't believe my life had turned into some kind of crime drama. My head swarmed and I felt like I was drowning. I'd spent an entire year trying to forget all the bad stuff and now I needed to remember it and write about it.

When we got home, Ellen and I went right to our bedroom to start writing. Ellen got her letters done in no time, but I wrote and rewrote and scribbled out and it took me all day to write a half page. I used my best cursive writing to recopy the letter to my mother. If it was going to be a legal document, I needed to make sure it was written neatly.

Dear Mom,

I just found out you were taking money that never belonged to you in the first place. That money belonged to Dad and it was supposed to be for me and Ellen. When I found this out, it upset me greatly. I know you felt as if there was nothing wrong with our family and I tried to think that also, but it's not true. Saul yelled at us all the time and you went along with everything he said. I know I've never come right out and said I don't want to live with you, but I'm saying it now. I don't want to hurt your feelings and I'm not saying I don't love you. You will always be my mother, but I want to stay in State College. This is my home now.

-Beth

Decades later, I will find this letter, in a box of legal papers hidden away in the attic of my aunt and uncle's house. My aunt saved copies of all the court proceedings and my letter was amongst the dusty documents.

Reading this letter as an adult will bring me to tears. The pain will not come from what the letter says, but all that it doesn't say. It will remind me of how afraid and desperate I felt. How I was beholden to my mother, even though I no longer lived under her reign. How I yearned for her approval and love. So much so, I couldn't even acknowledge how she allowed Saul to sexually abuse me and Ellen. Her betrayal was too much to commit to paper. There was no way for me to make sense of it all, so in order to survive I pushed it all away. I figured I could pretend it didn't really happen. But, it did happen. And I will spend a good portion of my adult life unpacking my memories, uncovering the source of my shame.

Chapter 40:
Our Day In Court

AT 9 O'CLOCK on a sunny July morning, we drove to the courthouse in a little town outside State College, called Bellefonte. Our court time was scheduled for 10 o'clock, but Uncle Benny thought we ought to be there early. My stomach was in knots. I'd been feeling all kinds of awful since writing the letters, one to the judge and the other to my mom. I hated having to go through all this and wanted the whole nightmare to be over.

Uncle Benny dropped me, Ellen and Auntie Esther off in front of the old white building, and then he went to park the car. The courthouse looked like something grand, with great big pillars and a bunch of steps leading to the front doors. Ellen and I held hands as we walked up the steps. We were both wearing new dresses Auntie Esther bought us for our day in court. I wore pantyhose for the first time in my life and they felt itchy against my skin.

When we got inside, Mr. Farley greeted us. He looked exactly the same as the first time I'd met him. Dark suit, hair parted on the side, baby face. He told us the judge would meet with Ellen first and then he'd meet with me.

"Why can't we go together?" I asked, panic seeping through my pores.

"He wants to hear from both of you separately. It's going to be okay, Beth, I promise."

Ellen and I sat on a hard wooden bench in the hallway waiting for the judge. Time passed slowly and it seemed like we'd been there for 15 hours instead of 15 minutes, when Mom and Saul walked through the front doors of the courthouse. Mr. Farley had told us they'd been invited to attend the hearing, but I never thought they'd actually show up. Mom's arm was wrapped around Saul's and it looked like she was having trouble walking. Her skin was pale and pasty. I wondered if her Multiple Sclerosis had gotten worse. I felt an overwhelming urge to cry.

A voice in my head said, "Don't cry. Be strong."

Mom walked over to us and gave us each a hug. She had the same smell, raw crescent roll dough.

"Don't cry. Be strong," the voice in my head chanted.

The judge came to get Ellen. He wasn't wearing a long black robe, like I'd imagined. He wore a dark suit, just like Mr. Farley's. I squeezed Ellen's hand before she followed the judge back to his chamber.

While Ellen was gone, Mom and Auntie Esther and Uncle Benny talked quietly. I couldn't even imagine what they were saying and I didn't want to know. I watched Saul pace back and forth up and down the long corridor, like a caged bull. A familiar fear crept up inside me and I felt like I couldn't breathe. I scurried into the bathroom, so I wouldn't have to look at him. I splashed some cold water on my face and ran my fingers through my long thick hair. I stayed in the bathroom, washing my hands and drying them in slow motion. Anything to avoid being in the same space as Saul. When I finally came out of the bathroom, I saw Ellen and the judge. Mr. Farley, Auntie Esther and Uncle Benny, Mom and Saul huddled around them. I stood three feet outside the group, always on the outside looking in.

Mom and Saul walked away first. Saul's lips were pursed in his usual angry way, but Mom looked different. Her eyes were filled with tears. I actually felt sorry for her. She walked toward me, kissed me on the head and said "Be good." Then she and Saul were gone.

I made my way over to the group and learned that the judge had awarded guardianship to my aunt and uncle, based solely on his meeting with Ellen. I was off the hook. Ellen couldn't protect me from Saul, but she'd saved me from having to testify. Her eyes were red and puffy. She hugged me tight. We'd finally found our home.

Chapter 41:
Bat Mitzvah Memories

Beth Schulman

I am happy to announce my Bat Mitzvah on the twenty-sixth day of June,
Nineteen hundred and eighty-two, at ten o'clock in the morning. I would hope you
will be able to attend and to share in the joy of the occasion with my family and me.
The service will take place at Congregation Brit Shalom,
620 East Hamilton Avenue, State College, Pennsylvania.
We invite you to join us at the Kiddush luncheon immediately after the service.

* * *

I HELD THE INVITATION at the corner between two fingers and
gently touched the royal blue cursive letters with my other hand.
Each letter was raised, as if written in Braille. My Bat Mitzvah invitation
didn't read like any others in the gigantic binder Auntie Esther and I
had pored over at the stationary store. All the other ones said things
like, "Mr. and Mrs. So and So are proud to announce, their lovely
daughter's Bat Mitzvah, *Blah Blah Blah.* I didn't have a Mom and Dad
announcing anything. Uncle Benny suggested I write my own invitation,
using my own words. I liked the idea of creating something unique
that was all mine.

I examined the front of the cushioned photo album, covered
with funny-looking fat cats. I'd never been much of a cat person, but
the photo album was a Bat Mitzvah present from one of Auntie
Esther's friends, so I figured I should use it. It came in its own shiny

ivory-colored box. I opened the album and pulled back the clear plastic on the first page. I secured the invitation in place and flattened the clear plastic sheet on top. I took the stack of photos from my Bat Mitzvah out of the Kodak envelope. Uncle Benny had picked them up from the Camera Shop that morning and they were still warm. I put one of the pictures against my cheek and it felt like it just came from the dryer. I spread the 24 photos on my bed so I could look at them all at once.

It was the end of July. Hard to believe it'd been only 3 weeks since my Bat Mitzvah day. Time crept so slowly when you were waiting for something big to happen, but once the something big happened, it became a distant memory in no time. There were several pictures of me and Rabbi Joel standing on the little stage in front of the synagogue called the *bemah*. This was where the entire service took place, in front of the 45 friends who attended. Most of the guests were friends of Auntie Esther and Uncle Benny, but my whole Sunday School class was there, too. Cindy and Liza sat right in the front row.

One picture caught my attention. I picked it up to get a closer look. Rabbi Joel was looking down at me. His mouth was open, as if he was right in the middle of saying something. My eyes were glued to his and I looked very serious in my A-line cotton dress, covered in little blue flowers and edged in white lace. My long hair was perfectly straight. I'd woken up early that morning, showered and patiently blew out my thick hair, layer by layer. I borrowed Brooke's curling iron to make my bangs curl right at my eyebrows. My satin headband matched the lace on my dress. Rabbi Joel wore a baby blue sports jacket, complimenting the blue in my dress, as if we'd planned our outfits together. His button-up shirt was as white as fresh snow and his bright yellow tie shined like a beam of sunshine. His yamakah was trimmed in gold stitching and sat on top of his head amongst his soft brown curls.

I remembered this moment more clearly than any other that day. Rabbi Joel had announced to the entire congregation that I was the first person, at the age of 13 to come to him and actually ask permission to learn Hebrew and read Torah. He explained that most Jewish children were forced to attend Hebrew School and become a Bar or Bat Mitzvah. He said I wasn't like most children. I'd made the conscious choice, to study and learn, and for that I should feel very proud.

When I looked real close at the picture I saw one little tear glistening on my cheek. I'm sure no one else noticed it, not even Rabbi Joel. That tear was for my dad. I'd imagined him sitting amongst the other guests, handkerchief in hand, wiping away his own tears of joy. I touched the little tear on my cheek in the picture. That tear was the first of many I'd shed for my dad in the coming years. It'd take much longer, over a decade in fact, to mourn the loss of my mom.

Epilogue

THERE HAVE BEEN several times in my life when I found myself mourning the relationship I never had with my mother. She'd missed all the milestones of my early adult life. She wasn't sitting amongst the other parents in the bleachers at my high school or college graduations. I didn't call her when I got engaged at the age of 26 or invite her to my wedding a year later.

The time I felt her absence most profoundly was when I became a new mother. My husband and I had just bought a small house at the end of a cul-de-sac in Horsham, Pennsylvania, a suburb of Philadelphia. The neighborhood was full of young families like us. The thing that sold me on the house was the mailbox. It stood out at the end of our driveway. It wasn't black like all the others on our cul-de-sac. The mailbox had brightly colored hearts and flowers stenciled on it and said *Welcome Home*. It wasn't gold, like the one my mother had painted so long ago, but it did make a statement.

When I was three months pregnant with baby number two, my 17-month-old son and I took our daily walk to the mailbox. This had become part of our afternoon routine. He'd wake from his nap and the first thing he'd say was *juice* followed by *mail*. I'd fill his Sippy cup with watered-down apple juice and he'd take it and race toward the door. He'd run down our driveway and stop at the mailbox. "*Uppy*," he'd say. This was my cue to lift him up so he could reach into our brightly decorated mailbox and pull out all the treasures nestled inside.

The mailbox was fuller than usual and my sweet baby squealed with delight. He reached his chubby hand in and grabbed as much mail as he could. One envelope fell to the ground. I gently placed him down, so I could retrieve the lost letter. A wave of nausea washed over me as I held the envelope with "Beth Schulman" written on the front in my mother's distinctive half print, half cursive handwriting. My hands started to shake as I opened it and carefully removed and unfolded the yellow lined paper.

Dear Ellen and Beth,

I hope this letter finds you both well.
There hasn't been one day, over the past 15 years, that I haven't thought about you.
I often wonder what you're doing with your lives and I hope you are both happy and healthy.
My MS has progressed to a point where I need to be in a wheelchair full time.
My health has declined over the last several years. I've been diagnosed with heart disease, diabetes and breast cancer. I'm sharing this information with you because it's important for you to know your family medical history. I hope you will take care of yourselves and I pray you remain healthy. I would love to resume a relationship with both of you. Saul doesn't know I'm writing to you, so if you do want to correspond (and I hope you do), please send your letter to my friend's house.
Her address is: 1914 Avenue K, Brooklyn, NY 11234

With much love, Mom

I read the letter a dozen times before deciding to write back. I had a sinking feeling my mother was at the end of her life and she didn't want to go to her grave with the guilt of all the pain she'd caused us. I assumed she wanted to clear her conscience and I wanted answers. I composed a letter summarizing where I was in my life and all I'd accomplished. I'd graduated college and went onto graduate school. I'd gotten my masters degree in education and was a kindergarten teacher in an affluent school district. I wanted her to know I'd made it, despite her abuse and absence. I ended with two questions I'd struggled with for years. *Why did you allow so many terrible things to happen to us? Why did you choose to devote yourself to an abusive tyrant, at the expense of your children?*

My mother wrote back soon after I sent the letter. She was happy to hear I was married and had one son, with another on the way. She admitted to making lots of mistakes when we were growing up and if she had it to do all over again, she'd do it differently. Not exactly an apology, but I decided it was enough. After all that had happened, I still yearned for a connection.

Over the next two months we corresponded through letters. I made photo albums of my wedding day and baby pictures of my son and sent them to her. We spoke on the phone once and made plans to see each other the following month in New York. Each time I walked into the kitchen, I found myself staring at the note I'd written on the calendar, *visit mom* written in a red fine tip marker.

One week before our scheduled visit, Saul called Auntie Esther to get Ellen's phone number. He called Ellen and told her our mother had died of a massive heart attack. Ellen called me.

"She's dead," Ellen said.

My heart sank deep into the pit of my stomach. When I hung up the phone, I walked slowly over to the calendar and put a big X over the words *visit mom*.

Then, I wept.

* * *

On June 17, 2014, I got a Facebook message from my mother's youngest brother. Her brother lived in southern California, not far from where he and my mother and their 3 other siblings grew up. I'd only met him a few times. His message said he wanted to visit me and Ellen. Without much thought, I nonchalantly replied that if he ever found himself in Pennsylvania, he should give me a call. I was shocked and somewhat alarmed when he called just a few days later, to tell me he'd booked a flight to Philadelphia and would be arriving in two weeks.

* * *

My uncle and I sat, knee-to-knee, on the overstuffed couch in my living room, sipping iced tea. We were virtual strangers and it took me awhile to work up the courage to ask the question I'd wondered about so much of my life. Finally, I took the last swig of my tea and asked, "What was life like for you and my mother when you were growing up?

He didn't hesitate. It was as if he'd been waiting all his life for this very moment, waiting to share the stories he'd buried for way too long. He told me how his parents got divorced when he was only a toddler. He explained that his father was an alcoholic and didn't have much of a relationship with him or his siblings. He told me how my mother yearned to have a relationship with their alcoholic father. When my grandmother got remarried, my mother was furious. She hated her stepfather. He was mean and controlling. My mother called him Hitler. My uncle got choked up when he described how his big sister, my mother, protected him from their stepfather's abuse. He told me how alone he felt, when my mother was sent away to live with an aunt in New York. Their mother had sent her away because she just couldn't get along with her stepfather. My grandmother chose the relationship with her new husband over the relationship with her daughter. It all sounded very familiar. I assumed there was more to the story, but I'd heard enough.

The story he shared didn't take away any of the pain and suffering I experienced as a child, nor did it justify my mother's actions. But having some insight into my mother's childhood, did allow me to feel something I'd never felt for her when she was alive. Empathy. Having empathy for my mother was the antidote to the shame I'd felt for so many years. I'll never completely forgive my mother for all she put me through, but I've been able to forgive myself. My empathy for her gave me the strength to let go of the anger that lurked within me for way too long. It gave me the courage to explore the dark places of my own childhood and write my story.

We're all shaped by our experiences. I wouldn't be the person I am today without having lived through the trauma of my childhood. It wasn't easy and there have been many hurdles along the way. But my past has brought me to the place I am today, a place of compassion, love and deep gratitude.

No one can go back and make a brand new start;
however, anyone can start from now
and make a brand new ending.

—MICHAEL BAISDEN

Author's Note

THE PROCESS of writing this book was painstaking at times, but in the end, sharing my story, has been cathartic and liberating. I, like so many adults of childhood neglect and abuse, spent the majority of my life trying to shed my backstory, like a snake sheds his skin. I wanted to fit in and just be normal. I attended college and graduate school, invested myself in a fulfilling career as a teacher, got married and started a family. When I had children of my own, the voices from my past came back to haunt me. I constantly second guessed myself as a new mother. Wondering how I could be a good mother when my own mother abandoned me. Telling my story allowed me to confront the demons from my past and helped me understand how they were effecting my present. This book is a tribute to all of you and your untold stories. Our stories shape who we are and what we become. They matter.

Loving ourselves through the process of owning our story is the bravest thing we'll ever do.

—**Brene' Brown**

"The consequences of abuse and neglect can be profound and can last long into the life cycle. However, once a child's safety is assured, thriving after abuse is possible."

—**Joyfulheartfoundation.org**

*All the names in this book have been changed, except for my own.

Acknowledgments

FIRST AND FOREMOST, I'd like to thank ,**Claire Bidwell Smith,** who had a huge impact on me and my writing. Claire, author of two stunning books **The Rules of Inheritance and After This,** believed in my story as soon as she read it. She supported and guided me through the complicated process of writing a book proposal. Thank you, Claire, for your unwavering kindness and encouragement.

To **Rachel Thompson, Justin Bogdanovitch, Melissa Flickinger, Wendy C. Garfinkle, Zee Hayat,** for all your help through this incredible process of book making. I'm overcome with gratitude and so proud to be associated with such a fine group of human beings.

To my dear friends and fellow writers, **Angela True** and **Sheri Johnson** for the countless hours we spent reading and responding to one another's work. You both have incredible stories and I can't wait to see your books in print.

To my fellow teachers at **Jarrettown Elementary School** for your undivided attention and positive feedback whenever I shared sample excerpts in the teacher's lunchroom.

To my colleagues at *The Penn Literacy Network,* especially **Bonnie Botel-Sheppard,** for always believing in me, even when I didn't believe in myself.

To the special man in my life, **Kenny Kury,** for being my number one cheerleader and occasional editor.

To all my friends and family, for your ongoing dedication to me and my book.

And to my dear sister for always loving and supporting me. You are my hero.

Questions and Topics for Discussion

1. Who would you identify as the hero in the story? Why?

2. Who would you consider more of a villain, Saul or Beth's mother, Gaye. Why?

3. What is your impression of Beth's father? Why do you think Beth and Ellen didn't tell him about the abuse?

4. Patti, Jenny's mom, helped Beth just by being kind to her. Can you think of a person in your life that made a difference through their kindness?

5. Do you think Patti knew what was going on in Beth's home? If you were Patti and suspected your child's friend was in an abusive/neglectful situation, what would you do?

6. Camp was Beth's safe haven. She writes, "The best part about camp was no one knew about your life back home. They didn't know your parents were divorced or you lived in the kitchen. They didn't know your mom had gone a little crazy." How would Beth's life have been different if she didn't go to camp? Did you have a place like this as a child? Is there a place that you can go that feels like a safe haven?

7. How did Beth's relationship with her sister, Ellen evolve and change throughout the story?

8. How would the story be different if told from Ellen's point of view?

9. If you were Beth, would you have wanted to regain a relationship with your mother? Why or why not?

10. Why do you think the book is called, The Gold Mailbox?

Interview with Beth Schulman, Author of The Gold Mailbox

JANUARY 20, 2016 / MELISSA FLICKS

Welcome Beth, tell us a little bit about yourself:

When I was 11 years old, I dreamed about the fairy tale life I'd have someday; a quaint arts and crafts style house, nestled on a cul-de-sac at the end of a tree lined street in the suburbs. My house would be filled with love and laughter, an adoring husband and children, lots of children.

This projected picture of my perfect life came from the endless hours I spent watching all the TV families I adored; The Waltons, The Cunnighams, The Huxtables. It was far from the real life I lived as an 11-year-old girl. I lived with a manic mother who suffered from multiple sclerosis and her abusive boyfriend in a house with no running water. While the TV kids had parents who drove them to soccer games and piano lessons on the weekends, my weekends were spent getting up before the sun rose to work at the flea markets with my emotionally distant mother and her hot headed boyfriend. When I grew up, I did achieve some of my earlier dreams-house, husband, children. But of course, it wasn't quite the fantasy I'd dreamed up as an 11-year-old girl. There have been many ups and downs, curves and turns in my adult life. I like so many adults of childhood neglect and abuse, have spent way too much time trying to shed my back-story, like a snake sheds his skin. Writing my story helped me come to terms with my childhood and embrace it. The following quote has been my guide.

"Life is not a matter of holding good cards, but of playing a poor hand well."
-Robert Louis Stevenson

It's no surprise that I've devoted my adult life to creating a safe and nurturing home for my two sons and a creative, supportive classroom for the students I teach. I've tried to give the children in my life the love, compassion and care I missed in my early years. I've got a Bachelor of Science Degree in Individual and family studies and a Master's Degree in Early Childhood and Elementary Education.

Where did you come up with the idea to write your book?

I'd spent much of my life trying to keep busy, always moving forward at warp speed, avoiding thoughts of my early years of abuse and neglect. It wasn't until I became a mother, that the voices from my past came back to haunt me. I was struggling in ways I couldn't explain or understand. As a form of therapy I started recording memories from my childhood. My writing was confined to a journal I took out mostly in the summertime when I had a reprieve from my job as a kindergarten teacher. Over many years the journal entries developed into scenes and the scenes into a story.

Fast-forward fifteen years – I was divorced and busy teaching kindergarten during the day and graduate students at night. The story I'd written about my childhood had been packed away in a box alongside the scrapbooks I'd started making when my babies were still babies. My two sons were almost fully-grown, living their own busy lives as high school students and athletes. I felt a new resolve to get my story finished. I dusted off my old journal and started taking writing courses and going on writer's retreats. I became completely immersed in getting my story out. I was determined to finish it. As I started sharing it with other writers and close friends, their enthusiasm and encouragement helped me gain the confidence to get it published.

Tell us about the title of the book and how it came about.

The Title of my book is The Gold Mailbox.

When my mother divorced my father she went through a crazy women's lib phase, rearranging our living room furniture every couple of days, hosting "consciousness raising meetings" in our apartment, and going out on dates that would last until the next morning. During this time, she painted our black mailbox, gold. She did this in one of her frenzied states and it was a sloppy mess. I was seven years old and it was the first time I can remember being really embarrassed by my mother's erratic behavior. So many changes were going on in my home, so many secrets. The gold mailbox became a neon sign announcing my mother's dysfunction to te entire neighborhood.

What is the hardest thing about writing?
For me, the hardest thing has been the process of revision and editing. I know how important this process is, but it can sometimes feel overwhelming. The more I read and reread my work, the more I wanted to cut and redo.

What advice would you give to aspiring writers?
Don't give up. If you're stuck, leave it alone for a few days. When you come back to it, you will see it in a whole new way.
Also, I found it really helpful to be part of a writer's group. Reading and responding to other people's writing, helped me become a better writer. Also, reading my work aloud to others became a powerful tool in figuring out what to keep, what to cut and what to rewrite.

What message (if any) are you trying to get across with your book?
I want my story to inspire readers to understand and "own" their stories. I lived so much of my life hiding from my past and feeling

deeply ashamed about it. Once I was able to unpackage and understand where my shame was coming from, I was able to feel "whole" and live a much healthier happier life. Our stories are important. They shape who we are and what we become.

Author Links

Facebook: Beth Schulman
Twitter: bschulmanauthor
Website: http://bethschulman.com
Email: Bethschulman2015@gmail.com

Beth loves hearing from readers.
Feel free to contact her to speak at your book club,
either in person or via Skype.